GATHEKAS

GATHEKAS

A Universalist Sufi Catechism

Modern Reader's Edition

Hazrat Pir-o-Murshid

Inayat Khan

Edited and Annotated by

Pir Netanel Miles-Yépez

The Inayati-Maimuni Order
Boulder, Colorado
2021

"The old shall be renewed,
and the new shall be made holy."
— Rabbi Avraham Yitzhak Kook

Albion-Andalus, Inc.
P. O. Box 19852
Boulder, CO 80308
www.albionandalus.com

Design and composition by Albion-Andalus Books
Cover design by D.A.M. Cool Graphics
Cover image: "Rose Heart and Wings" by Netanel Miles-Yépez.
Mehndi design used from Vecteezy.com

ISBN-13: 978-1-7348750-7-2 (HC)
ISBN-13: 978-1-953220-08-0 (PB)

Manufactured in the United States of America

Toward the One
The Perfection of Love, Harmony, and Beauty
The Only Being
United with all the Illuminated Souls
Who form the Embodiment of the Message
The Spirit of Guidance

CONTENTS

Editor's Preface

Among the oral teachings of Hazrat Inayat Khan (1882-1927), collected and transcribed for private use by his murids, the *Gathekas* were specifically intended for *taliban*, or 'candidates' for initiation into the Sufi path. The Sanskrit word, *gāthikā*, refers to an epic poem or sacred song, and is consistent with the other music and poetry related titles he gave to most of his more focused teachings for murids. In this case, these are teachings meant to help seekers understand the fundamentals of the Sufi Message and the nature of the Sufi path.

In his *Sangithas*, Inayat Khan made it clear that he wished the candidate to "meditate" upon these teachings, and not to study them in the way of conventional Western education. The *Gathekas*, he says . . .

> are as a line to tread upon. As one follows that line, one observes different things necessary to be observed on the spiritual path. For instance, a map of a city shows different roads that lead to different places; but by traveling those roads, you will see for yourself interesting sights to ponder and appreciate, and by the help of which you may accomplish your purpose in life.

That is to say, you must learn how to benefit from these teachings in your everyday life, and to see for yourself the beauty and complexity that may be found there, precisely "by following those lines that are as roads leading to the desired goal." The *Gathekas* are thus to be 'contemplated' in the context of your life and not 'studied' in the dispassionate and disinterested mode of Western education.

I have chosen not to provide commentary on the *Gathekas* here, hoping to leave the text open for fresh discussion and interpretation. However, I have included a number of notes to assist the general reader in a few places, providing occasional historical and cultural context, and information that may be helpful for understanding obscure names and references made by Inayat Khan.

While the work of Inayat Khan is certainly universalist and egalitarian, he nevertheless spoke, according to the conventions of his day, using the masculine 'he' as inclusive of the feminine 'she,' and in an English that might seem somewhat archaic today. Moreover, most of his so-called 'writings' are actually transcriptions of oral talks, collected and edited by his disciples. Thus, they include many repetitions, excurses, abrupt changes of subject, and occasional mistakes. In reading a passage in the original edition it may become clear to the discerning reader that one sentence does not necessarily follow from the previous sentence, and the larger context may actually make it obvious that there is an error in the text. For instance, in the original version of Gatheka XXIX, we read . . .

> The whole thing is to meet one's condition with understanding and with complete resignation that one shall not improve one's condition. No, the first thing is to meet the condition as it is, and the second thing is to better the condition. The less conflict one can use in it the better; the more one can avoid the conflict, the better it is.

The first sentence is given like a definite prescription, and then contradicted by the following sentence. It is likely that this is the result of a simple (but important) omission of the word 'not'—"The whole thing is *not* to meet one's condition with understanding and with complete resignation that one shall not improve one's condition."

Preface

For this and many other reasons, I have chosen to re-edit the *Gathekas* for clarity in modern English, rendering its often long complex sentences and obscure phrases into simpler, more direct statements, while also making them gender inclusive, in accord with current values. Thus, in the Modern Reader's Edition, the previous passage has been reconstructed to show what we believe is the original intention of Inayat Khan in a clear, modern English:

> It is not our goal to become resigned to the fact that we will never improve our circumstances in life; but we must first come to terms with our circumstances *as they are* before attempting to improve them. The less conflict there is in the process, the better.

Despite such edits, I believe these *Gathekas* may still be read as the words of Inayat Khan, and still represent his intentions. Indeed, they may actually represent his intentions more clearly than the original. Nevertheless, because I have made these adjustments to the language, it must be understood that this edition is necessarily an interpretation of the original, made according to the best of my own understanding and liable to error. Thus, I must take full responsibility for any errors I may have introduced in it. If those errors are few, it is owing to the proofreading and careful editing suggestions of my student, Daniel Jami, who also assembled the basic glossary terms and index.

Netanel Mu'in ad-Din Miles-Yépez
Boulder, Colorado, December 10th, 2020

"As the rose blooms amidst thorns,
so great souls shine out through all opposition."
— *The Bowl of Saqi*

GATHEKA I
What is Sufism?

What is meant by the word 'Sufi'?

The word 'Sufi' is derived from the Arabic word *safa*, which literally means, 'pure.'[1] That is to say, the Sufi is pure from distinctions and differences. Thus, it may also be derived from the Greek word *sophos*, meaning 'wise.'

Sufism cannot be called deism, for the Sufi does not consider God to be a separate entity.[2] Neither can it be called pantheism, because the Sufi sees the immanence of God in nature, but also realizes God's essence in the infinite, naming God, Allah, the Formless, the Colorless.[3] The Sufi is not a believer in the unrealized God, nor an unbeliever in the idealized God, and is thus distinguished from godly and ungodly alike. The Sufi is not an atheist, for the Sufi denies neither God, nor God's messengers.[4]

To the questions, 'Are you a Muslim? A Christian? or a Jew?' *et cetera*, the Sufi's answer would be 'Yes' rather than 'No,' for the Sufi opposes no religion, but sympathizes with all. In fact, Sufism cannot be called a 'religion,'[5] for it does not impose either belief or principle upon anyone; each individual soul has its own principles best suited to it and a belief that changes with each grade of evolution.

Sufism is not an intellectual philosophy, because it does not depend upon cold reasoning, but develops a devotional tendency. Sufism cannot be called occult, for the Sufi does not attribute any importance to the investigation of supernatural

1

phenomena. Seeing the brevity of life, a Sufi deems this a worthless pursuit. The Sufi's aim is God alone.

The Origin of Sufism

The germ of Sufism is said to have existed from the beginning of human existence, for wisdom is the heritage of all.[6] Therefore, no one person can be said to be its progenitor. It has been revealed more clearly and spread more widely from time-to-time as the world has evolved.

Sufi fellowships may be traced back as far as the period of the prophet Daniel.[7] We find among the Zoroastrians, Hatim, the best known Sufi of his time. The chosen of God, the salt of the earth, who responded without hesitation to the call of Abraham, Moses, Jesus, and Muhammad, were all Sufis. They were not merely simple followers of a religion, but also had insight into divine knowledge. They recognized all of God's messengers and united with them all. Before the time of Muhammad, they were called the *Ikhwan as-Safa*, the 'fellowship of purity.' But after his coming, they were named by him, *Sahab-i Safa*, 'knights of purity.' It is only the world that has called them Zoroastrian, Christian, Jewish, or Muslim mystics.

The followers of each religion have claimed them as their own. For instance, a Christian would claim that Paul of Tarsus was a Christian, and a Muslim that Shams-i Tabriz was a Muslim. In reality, Jesus was not a Christian, nor was Muhammad a Muslim—they were both Sufis.

Relation to Other Religions

Although Sufism is the essence of all religions and its influence is upon all, it can more justly be called the esoteric side of Zoroastrianism, Judaism, Christianity, and Islam. But it is not a purely Zoroastrian esotericism devoid of Jewish influence, nor is it a solely Jewish mysticism free from the influence of Christianity, nor is it entirely Christian wisdom untouched by the morals of Islam. Therefore, it is justifiable to call it the true spirit of all religions, even of those as foreign to it as the Hindu Vedanta and Buddhism.[9]

We see Zarathustra (Zoroaster) in the Sufi's purity, their love of light and worship of God in the sublimity of nature. We see Moses in the Sufi's constant communion with God. We see Christ in the Sufi's charity and self-renunciation. The true meaning of the sacrament is seen in the daily life of the Sufi, who readily shares all with another. The life of a true Sufi is a Bible open for anyone to read. We see Muhammad in the humanity of the Sufi, in their strength in facing the struggle of life and bearing with equanimity its responsibilities.

The Sufi Message

Sufism was intellectually born in Arabia, devotionally reared in Persia, and spiritually completed in India.[10] For the last forty years, the direct and indirect influence of the East has prepared the ground in the West for the seed of the Sufi Message.[11] Every event has its time, and it has been ordained by the supreme will that East and West shall now unite in the bond of love and wisdom, which neither politics nor commerce can bring about, but only the call of God, the sovereign of both East and West.

Notes on Gatheka I

1. *The word 'Sufi' is derived from the Arabic word* safa, *which literally means, 'pure.'*

The consensus view is that the word 'Sufi' is actually derived from the Arabic, *suf,* meaning 'wool.' This was probably a descriptive appellation that arose in a time when the average Muslim was just becoming aware of a curious group of Muslim spiritual seekers on the margins of society, wearing woolen robes as a symbol of their values and as an ascetic spiritual practice. Thus, people called them *sufiyya,* 'wool-wearers.' Some believe that this practice of wearing wool may have begun

3

in imitation of Christian hermits in the deserts of the Near and Middle East during the early period of Islam's formation. In that time, in those generally arid environs, to wear rough woolen garments was a powerful declaration for the 'life of the spirit' over that of 'the flesh' (which no doubt chaffed under the coarse wool). For the Essenes, the Desert Parents, and these early Sufis, the rough and tattered wool cloak *(khirqah)* was a badge of spiritually self-imposed poverty, of a life of simplicity dedicated exclusively to God-seeking.

Others have suggested that the word 'Sufi' is connected with the Arabic word *suffah*, 'bench.' To many, the appearance and behavior of the early Sufis brought to memory those who were called the 'People of the Bench.' These were a band of poor and homeless followers of the prophet Muhammad who slept on a bench outside the mosque in Medina, sharing whatever food and possessions they had with one another. This sense of 'homelessness,' living solely on God's providence, is another potent symbol for the Sufi, whose way is to become free from attachment to sense objects, finding the only true home in the heart.

The Muslim philosopher al-Biruni (d. 1048 C.E.) offered an explanation of the term 'Sufi' which is more expressive of accomplishment, relating it to the Greek word, *sophos*, meaning 'wise.' Hazrat Pir-o-Murshid Inayat Khan supports this view and other such explanations, telling us in early editions of the *Gathekas* that the word Sufi "comes from a Persian word meaning wisdom," among whose kin is the Greek word *sophia*, also designating "wisdom." (Gatheka IV, XXI, XXII)

But perhaps the most significant etymologies for the Sufi come from the Arabic words, *safwa*, meaning the 'chosen ones," and *safa*, meaning 'pure." Using both of these to speak of the Sufis, the master Abu'l Qasim al-Qushayri (d. 1074 C.E.) says:

> They were *the chosen* among God's friends, honored above other worshippers after the messengers and prophets ... and purified from all obscurities.

"Chosen" has the sense of being *chosen to be purified* and reflects the gratitude of the recipient of divine grace. Likewise, the purity of *safa* is not a boast, but is both prescriptive and reflective of a spiritual state, as Inayat Khan says, "pure from distinctions and differences."

GATHEKA I

2. Sufism cannot be called deism, for the Sufi does not consider God to be a separate entity.

Inayat Khan's use of "deism" is not to be confused with the 'deism' of the 17th- and 18th-century Enlightenment philosophers. That deism emphasized a God, often compared to a "clockmaker," that creates and sets the universe in motion, but takes no further part in it.

3. Neither can it be called pantheism, because the Sufi sees the immanence of God in nature, but also realizes God's essence in the infinite, naming God, Allah, the Formless, the Colorless.

Inayat Khan is referring to the pantheism of Barukh Spinoza and his notion of *deus sive natura*, God as indistinguishable from nature. This, however, is not pantheism as understood in Indian philosophy, where God is truly *All*, fully immanent and transcendent, as most Sufis believe.

4. The Sufi is not a believer in the unrealized God, nor an unbeliever in the idealized God, and is thus distinguished from godly and ungodly alike. The Sufi is not an atheist, for the Sufi denies neither God, nor God's messengers.

This is another way of stating the most important phrase of Muslims and Sufis alike, *Lā 'ilāha 'illā 'llāh.* For the average Muslim, this might be translated, 'There is no god, but God,' but, for the Sufi, this is better translated, 'There is no God; nevertheless, God.' There is no god to be found anywhere in our world; we look and find nothing. And yet, for some, there is a 'nevertheless,' an experience of the sacred that is undeniable. Thus, the Sufi honors the experience of both the atheist and the theist alike.

5. To the questions, 'Are you a Muslim? A Christian? or a Jew?' et cetera, the Sufi's answer would be 'Yes' rather than 'No,' for the Sufi opposes no religion, but sympathizes with all. In fact, Sufism cannot be called a 'religion' . . .

Consider the audacious suggestion of 'Ayn al-Quzat Hamadani:

O friend! If you would see what the Christians see in Jesus, you too would become a Christian! And if you would see what the Jews see in Moses, you too would become a Jew! Even more, if you would see what idol-worshippers see in idol-worship, you too would become and idol-worshipper! The seventy-two paths *(mazhab-ha)* are all way stages on the road to God. *(A Pearl in Wine.* New Lebanon, NY: Omega Publications, 2001: 244).

Sufism is not a religion, in as much as a religion is a social construct formed around the primary experience of a spiritual pathfinder. Thus, a religion, at its best, is a reconstruction of the original path taken by that pathfinder toward a primary experience of the sacred, hoping to help others to find their way to that experience as well. Unfortunately, in most cases, the religion becomes an end in itself and not a means. It becomes another idol to be broken. Sufism is a path of primary experience, and thus, is *not* a religion.

6. *The germ of Sufism is said to have existed from the beginning of human existence, for wisdom is the heritage of all.*

This conception of Sufism as a perennial wisdom (stemming from the Islamic conception of Adam as the first prophet) is found throughout Sufi literature, though Inayat Khan was one of the few, as well as one of the first, to follow this concept to its logical, universalistic conclusions.

7. *Sufi fellowships may be traced back as far as the period of the prophet Daniel.*

It is unclear what Inayat Khan is referring to here, whether that the prophet Daniel was a member of such a fellowship—perhaps with Hanani'ah (Shadrach), Misha'el (Meshach), and Azari'ah (Abednego)—or that these fellowships may be traced to the 5th-century B.C.E. (according to the biblical tradition) in Babylon. The reference to Zoroastrianism that follows may also be a clue to understanding this remark, given the history of the Magi in that period.

8. *But after his coming, they were named by him,* Sahab-i Safa, *'knights of purity.'*

The word "knights" is significant here, for much of Sufism is concerned with the practice of *adab,* 'etiquette,' and *futuwwah,* 'chivalry.'

9. *Therefore, it is justifiable to call it the true spirit of all religions, even of those as foreign to it as the Hindu Vedanta and Buddhism.*

The latter two are separated out because they are themselves "esoteric schools," as Inayat Khan will make clear in later gathekas.

10. *Sufism was intellectually born in Arabia, devotionally reared in Persia, and spiritually completed in India.*

That is to say that the historical origins of Sufism are found in Arabia, but the particular devotional, love-oriented emphasis of Sufism is cultivated in Persia. Later, the four major schools of Sufism (Chishti, Qadiri, Suhrawardi, Naqshbandi) come together in India, where Sufism becomes a truly universalist path.

11. *For the last forty years, the direct and indirect influence of the East has prepared the ground in the West for the seed of the Sufi Message.*

This may suggest a subversive understanding of Western colonization of the East, and of Orientalist interests, as creating the bridge or means by which Sufism and other spiritual traditions are spiritually and positively colonizing the West.

12. *Every event has its time, and it has been ordained by the supreme will that East and West shall now unite in the bond of love and wisdom, which neither politics nor commerce can bring about . . .*

This period witnessed World War I, the birth of the League of Nations, and the major manifestations of Communism and Capitalism as movements in the East and West.

GATHEKA II
Sufism—The Spirit of All Religions

The word '*sufi*,' or '*safa*,' implies purity, which contains two qualities. That which is pure is unmixed with any other element; in other words, purity exists in its own element, unalloyed and unstained. Secondly, what is pure is most adaptable. Pure water, for instance, is water without anything else in it; the test of its purity is that it can adapt itself to whatever is mixed with it. If it is mixed with a red powder, it becomes red, if with a green powder, green.

Such is the nature of the Sufi. In the first place, Sufis purify themselves by keeping the vision of God before them always, not allowing the stains of earthly differences and distinctions to be mirrored upon their hearts. Neither good nor bad society, nor dealings with people of high or low class, nor faith or belief can ever interfere with one's purity.

The Sufi demonstrates a universal kinship or fellowship through adaptability. Among Christians, one is a Christian. Among Jews, one is a Jew. Among Muslims, a Muslim. Among Hindus, a Hindu. A Sufi is with all, and thus, all are with the Sufis. Sufis allow everyone to join them in fellowship, and in the same way, allow themselves to join any other. The Sufi never questions, 'What is your creed, nation, or religion?' Neither does a Sufi ask, 'What are your teachings or principles?' If you call a Sufi 'sister' or 'brother,' they answer as a sister or a brother.

The Sufi has no fixed principles, because what is sweet may be beneficial to one and harmful to another. It is thus with all principles, good or bad, kind or cruel. If you require soldiers to be merciful during a battle, they will at once be defeated. Each person has their own principles for each action and situation.

The Sufi is a true Christian in life, charity, kinship, and in healing one's own soul, as well as that of another. The Sufi is not bigoted in adherence to a particular Christian sect, or in forsaking the masters who came before and after Christ; but the Sufi's attunement with Christ, their appreciation and practice of truth, are as keen as those of a true Christian. In the lives of the dervishes,[1] one sees the picture of the life and teachings of Jesus Christ, especially in that they share their food and abode with others, whether they be friend or foe. Even to this day, they continue in these ways. The Sufi is a Catholic in producing the picture of the ideal of devotion in one's soul. The Sufi is a Protestant in giving up many trappings of ritual.

The Sufi is a Brahmin, for the word 'brahmin' means knower of *Brahman,* God, the only being.[2] The Sufi's religion lies in believing in no other existence than that of God, which the Brahmin calls *advaita,* 'non-dual.'[3] The Sufi has as many grades of spiritual evolution to go through as does the Yogi.[4] There is very little difference in their practice, the difference being chiefly in name. Of course, the Sufi chooses a life in the world instead of an ascetic life, but does not restrict either the former or the latter. The Sufi considers the teachings of the avatars as true manifestations of divine wisdom, and is in perfect sympathy with the subtle knowledge of *vedanta.*[5]

The Sufi appreciates the Jain conception of 'harmlessness,' and considers kindness the only true path of purity and perfection.[6] Shams-i Tabriz, the Shiva of Persia,[7] fed maggots from his decaying flesh, the maggots growing larger and larger as they devoured it; and if he, while walking, saw any of them fall, he would pick them up and place them again upon his body, saying, "Your food has been created in this flesh." Later, he was flayed alive because he had been accused of declaring that the Godhead existed in his mortal body. From the past to the present, Sufis have shown great renunciation in their lives. Now, most of them are as Jains or Brahmins, leading a most harmless life.

The Sufi is Muslim without a doubt, not only because many Muslims are Sufis, or because they use the vocabulary of Islam, but because a Sufi proves in their life what a true Muslim is, and what the heart of the true Muslim ought to be. Muslims have so much devotion that, no matter how great a sinner or how cruel a person might be, the name of Allah or Muhammad at once reduces them to tears. Islam prepares one to be a Sufi.[8] The practices of Sufism develop the heart qualities that are often overlooked by other mystics. It is the purification of the heart that makes it fit for illumination from the soul.[9] The prophet Muhammad prophesied, "There will be seventy-two diverse classes of people among those who will walk in my light, but among them, there will be only one that will surely find their way." This is applied to the Sufi because it is they who read the Qur'an from every experience in life, and see and recognize Muhammad's face in each atom of manifestation.[10]

The Sufi is a Buddhist, for the Sufi reasons with every step on the spiritual journey. The teachings of the Sufis are akin to those of the Buddhists. In fact, it is the Sufi who unites believers in God with those who do not believe through the knowledge of unity.

The Sufi, as a Zoroastrian or a Parsi, looks toward the sun and bows before the air, fire, water, and earth, recognizing the immanence of God in God's manifestation, taking the sun, moon, and stars as signs of God. The Sufi interprets fire as the symbol of wisdom, and the sun as the celestial light. The Sufi not only bows before them, but also absorbs their quality.[11] As a rule, in the presence of dervishes, a wood fire and incense burn continually.

The Sufi is an Israelite or Jew, especially in the study of the different names of God, and the mastery of them. At the same time, the miraculous powers of Moses can be seen in the lives of Sufis past and present. The Sufi, in fact, is the master of Jewish mysticism.[12] The divine voice heard on Mount Sinai is audible to a Sufi today.

Notes on Gatheka II

1. *In the lives of the dervishes . . .*

Dervish is an Anglicized version of the Persian (Farsi) word, *darvish*, meaning, one who waits by the door or on the threshold; that is to say, a beggar. As with the Arabic word, *faqir*, 'poor one,' *darvish* is a positive term in the Sufi context, for 'poor' and 'beggar' both refer in Sufism to the self-emptying process of a Sufi, reducing the size of one's ego, hollowing out a place for God within.

2. *The Sufi is a Brahmin, for the word* 'brahmin' *means knower of* Brahman, *God, the only being.*

In the *varna*, or 'caste' system of the Hindu tradition, Brahmins are priests, the first and highest caste. Inayat Khan seems to use the term more generally as the seeker of *Brahman* as a non-dual reality.

3. *The Sufi's religion lies in believing in no other existence than that of God, which the Brahmin calls* advaita, *'non-dual.'*

Advaita is Sanskrit for 'not-two' or 'non-dual.' Advaita Vedanta is a Hindu philosophical school adopting an uncompromising position of absolute non-duality, just as Inayat Khan has described above.

4. *The Sufi has as many grades of spiritual evolution to go through as does the Yogi.*

A Yogi (Sanskrit, 'disciplined') is a spiritual practitioner of the meditative discipline called Yoga.

5. *The Sufi considers the teachings of the avatars as true manifestations of divine wisdom, and is in perfect sympathy with the subtle knowledge of* vedanta.

Avatar is Sanskrit for 'incarnation' and refers to the different manifestations of God, some of them in human form. In the Hindu tradition, these include Rama and Krishna. However, in his prayer "Salat," Inayat Khan includes them among the prophets.

The Sanskrit *vedanta* ('end of the Vedas') refers to the ultimate teaching of the Hindu *Veda*, called *Upanishad;* in this case, "the subtle knowledge of *vedanta*" is probably referring to the non-dual teachings of Advaita Vedanta.

6. *The Sufi appreciates the Jain conception of 'harmlessness,' and considers kindness the only true path of purity and perfection.*

The central tenet of Jainism is *ahimsa*, 'not-harming.' The tradition was established by Mahavira, who is thought to have been a contemporary of Siddhartha Gautama, the Buddha.

7. *Shams-i Tabriz, the Shiva of Persia . . .*

In referring to Shams-i Tabriz as the "Shiva of Persia," Inayat Khan is likely saying that Shams was the ideal of the untamed Yogi. Shiva, an *avatar* or manifestation of the divine reality in Hindu spirituality, is often talked about by Inayat Khan as a prophet in the Islamic sense.

8. *Islam prepares one to be a Sufi.*

Islam means 'surrender.' A Muslim is 'one who has surrendered.' Surrendering to God "prepares one to be a Sufi."

9. *It is the purification of the heart that makes it fit for illumination from the soul.*

Sufism is an Anglicized version of the Arabic, *tasawwuf*, meaning 'purification.'

10. *This is applied to the Sufi because it is they who read the Qur'an from every experience in life, and see and recognize Muhammad's face in each atom of manifestation.*

This is not a reference to the historical prophet, Muhammad, but to the Sufi conception of the *Nur-i Muhammad*, the 'light of Muhammad,' the perfected human ideal which existed before creation, and for which God brought everything into being.

11. *The Sufi interprets fire as the symbol of wisdom, and the sun as the celestial light. The Sufi not only bows before them, but also absorbs their quality.*

This Zoroastrian quality in Sufism is borne out in Inayat Khan's prayer, called, "Nayaz."

12. *The Sufi, in fact, is the master of Jewish mysticism.*

It seems likely that Inayat Khan had some exposure to Jewish mysticism *(kabbalah)*, probably through his American *murid*, Murshida Rabia Martin.

GATHEKA III
Sufism—Beyond Religion

Modern writers have often made mistakes in describing Sufism as a 'Persian philosophy,' or the 'esoteric side of Islam.' Some have erroneously believed it to have been influenced by Vedanta or Buddhism. Some Muslims have patriotically called it 'an outcome of Islam' to secure the credit for their own religion, while some Christians have attempted to win it for Christianity.

In fact, according to the sacred history Sufis have inherited from one another, Sufism has never been owned by any race or religion, for differences and distinctions are the very delusions from which Sufis purify themselves. It may appear that Sufism must have been formed of different elements of various religions prominent today, but it is not so, for Sufism itself is the essence of all the religions, as well as the spirit of Islam.

Sufism reveals all the shades and colors that represent the various religions of the world, having no particular color itself. All prophets, saints, sages, and mystics are owned by their followers, as Jesus is by Christians and Moses by Jews. Yet Jesus was not a 'Christian,' nor Moses a 'Jew,' both being Sufis, pure from earthly distinctions. The beloved of God are even as God, impervious to religious dogmas and principles.

Sufism is not a religion or a philosophy; it is neither deism nor atheism, nor is it a moral or a special kind of mysticism, being free from the usual religious sectarianism. If it could be called a religion, it would be a religion of love, harmony, and beauty. It could be called a philosophy, but it is beyond philosophy, because a Sufi, through the study of metaphysics, escapes the selfishness produced by philosophy and kindles the fire of devotion with eyes open to reason and logic.[1] The Sufi prays to Allah in every moment, invoking God's name, and realizing at the same time that the self is none other than God. For, to a Sufi, God is not a personal being, but a mighty healer awakening the soul from its delusion of earthly individuality, and a guide leading it to self-realization, the only aim in life.

The Sufi, by learning the greatest of all morals—*love*—arrives at the stage of self-abnegation, wherein one is liberated from all earthly morals. Mysticism has several aspects, but the Sufi strives toward the path of truth, its ultimate goal. The truth of the Sufi is the Truth common to all religions and philosophies, the realization of which grants salvation, or *najat*. Sufism, being the first fellowship of purity, has been known under different names, such as the 'knighthood of purity,' or the 'fellowship of the cave,' on which several other institutions have established kinships under different names.[2]

Notes on Gatheka III

1. *It could be called a philosophy, but it is beyond philosophy, because a Sufi, through the study of metaphysics, escapes the selfishness produced by philosophy and kindles the fire of devotion with eyes open to reason and logic.*

The non-dual mystical philosophies of our traditions systematically dismantle the foundations of the false self.

2. *Sufism, being the first fellowship of purity, has been known under different names, such as the 'knighthood of purity,' or the 'fellowship of the cave,' on which several other institutions have established kinships under different names.*

The point, again, is that the name, 'Sufism,' is not important. There is a famous saying among Sufis, "Once, Sufism was a reality without a name, now, it is a name without a reality."

GATHEKA IV
SUFISM—THE WISDOM OF ALL FAITHS

The word *'Sufi'* suggests 'wisdom.' From the original root, many derivations may be traced. Among the possible origins, the Greek *sophia*, 'wisdom,' is one of the most interesting.[1]

Wisdom is the ultimate power. In wisdom is rooted religion, which connects law and inspiration. But the point of view of the wise differs from that of the simple followers of a religion. The wise, whatever their faith, have always been able to meet beyond the boundaries of external form and convention, natural and necessary to human life, but which nonetheless separate humanity.

People of the same thought and point-of-view are drawn to each other with a tendency to form an exclusive circle. A minority is apt to fence itself off from the crowd. So it has been with mystics. Mystical ideas are unintelligible to people in general. Mystics have, therefore, usually imparted their ideas to a chosen few, those whom they could trust, who were ready for initiation and discipleship. Thus, great Sufis have appeared at different times and have founded schools of thought. Their expression of wisdom has differed to suit their different environments; but their understanding of life has been one and the same. The same herb planted in different atmospheric conditions will vary in form accordingly, but will retain its basic characteristics.

Historians sometimes trace the history of Sufism by noting the actual occurrence of the word, *'sufi,'* and by referring only to those schools which have definitely wished to be known by this name.[2] Some scholars find the origin of this philosophy in the teachings of Islam; others connect it with Buddhism.[3] Others do not reject as impossible the Semitic tradition that Sufism's foundation is to be attributed to the teachings of Abraham.[4] Many believe it arose around the same time as the teachings of Zarathustra (Zoroaster). Every age of the world has seen awakened souls, and, as it is impossible to limit wisdom to any one period or place, so it is impossible to date the origin of Sufism.

Not only have there been illuminated souls in all times, but there have been times when a wave of illumination has passed over humanity as a whole.[5] We believe that such a period is at hand. The calamity through which the world has lately passed,[6] and the difficult problems of the present, are due to the existence of borders; this fact is already clear to many. Sufism removes the borders that divide different faiths by bringing into full light the underlying wisdom which unites them.

Notes on Gatheka IV

1. The word 'Sufi' suggests 'wisdom.' From the original root, many derivations may be traced. Among the possible origins, the Greek sophia, 'wisdom,' is one of the most interesting.

See the earlier discussion of the etymology of the word 'Sufi' in the commentary on Gatheka I.

2. Historians sometimes trace the history of Sufism by noting the actual occurrence of the word, 'sufi,' and by referring only to those schools which have definitely wished to be known by this name.

Inayat Khan, and Sufis in general, find this view problematic. This is the history of a name, not the reality behind the name. The reality is not so limited.

GATHEKA IV

3. *Some scholars find the origin of this philosophy in the teachings of Islam; others connect it with Buddhism.*

Some connections between Sufis and Buddhists are suggested in the works of J. G. Bennett, *Gurdjieff: Making a New World* and *The Masters of Wisdom*.

4. *Others do not reject as impossible the Semitic tradition that Sufism's foundation is to be attributed to the teachings of Abraham.*

From one perspective, Sufism may be seen as a broadly Semitic mystical tradition whose ultimate origins are to be found in Abraham, the progenitor of all three Abrahamic faiths—Judaism, Christianity, and Islam. There is some historical support for this view.

5. *Not only have there been illuminated souls in all times, but there have been times when a wave of illumination has passed over humanity as a whole.*

The philosopher Karl Jaspers spoke of such times as "axial ages." The time of the Buddha, Mahavira, Lao Tzu, Socrates, and the great literary prophets of the Bible was such an age.

6. *The calamity through which the world has lately passed . . .*

This is a reference to World War I.

GATHEKA V
DIFFERENT SCHOOLS OF SUFISM

Sufism is the old school of quietism,[1] an ancient school of wisdom that was the origin of many cults of a mystical and philosophical nature. As the origin of all the occult and mystical schools is the ancient school of Egypt,[2] so Sufism has always represented that school, and has worked-out its destiny in the realm of quietude.

From Sufism came four schools.[3] The first was the Naqshbandi school, which worked with symbol, ritual, and ceremony. The second was the Qadiri school, which taught wisdom in the realm of the existing religion of the East. The third was the Suhrawardi school, which taught the mystery of life by the knowledge of metaphysics and the practice of self-control. The fourth was the Chishti school, which represented the spiritual ideal in the realm of poetry, music, *et cetera*. From these schools, many branches grew in Arabia, Turkey, Tartary, Russia, Turkestan, Bokhara, Afghanistan, India, Siberia, and other parts of Asia.

With the different schools the ideal remained the same, but the method differed. The main ideal of the Sufi has been to attain that perfection which Jesus Christ taught—"Be you perfect as your heavenly parent is perfect." (Matt. 5:48)[4] The method of the Sufi has always been that of self-effacement; but the effacement of which self? Not the real Self, but the false self on which we often depend, priding ourselves on being 'something,' in order to allow that real Self to manifest in the world of appearances. Thus, the Sufi method works toward the unfolding of the soul, the Self which is eternal, to which all power and beauty belong.

The Sufi Order

The Sufi Order represents the embodiment of all the schools and answers the need of the present day.[5] The Sufi Order, therefore, is the body composed of those interested in spiritual attainment, initiated in the order formed in 1910, when the Sufi Message was brought to the Western world.[6]

The Sufi path has Three Objects and Ten Thoughts.[7] The rights of initiates in the Sufi Order are the same all over the world.[8] The Sufi Order is constituted of an outer body as well as an inner spirit. As an outer body, it has its *khanqah* and its branches.[9]

The inner working of the order is regulated in the following way. There are four circles of initiates: the study circle, the advanced circle, the inner circle, and the higher circle.[10] One passes gradually through these by initiation. When one is designated a 'Sufi,' the obligation to the group is finished.[11] Then, if one wishes to continue to help humanity, one is authorized and initiated to work in that direction as a *khalif,* the 'deputy' of the spiritual guide, or as a *murshid,* the 'guide.'[12]

Every initiated 'seeker' or *murid* is trusted with certain exercises or teachings.[13] The *murid* is expected to keep the vow of secrecy, and to keep these not only from non-initiates, but also from other initiates.[14] An exercise is a prescription meant for a particular person, and that person cannot pass it on to another.[15] Initiation is a trust that a *murshid* gives to a *murid,* expecting sincerity from them. Trust and confidence empowers the *murid,* enabling them to proceed in the spiritual journey. The study of a certain philosophy is not enough; there must be sincerity behind it.[16] Sincerity must be the first thing in the path of spirituality. Jesus Christ called this "faith."

The Sufi Message

In all periods of the history of the world, and in all ancient traditions, one finds traces of a sacred 'call' given to different communities, nations, races, and the world-at-large. In the Qur'an, it is said, "We have sent our messengers to every part of the Earth, that they may not say they were not warned in time."[18] (57:25; 17:15) All traditions declare that a messenger is given to the world at the time of the world's need.[19]

People have given an unnecessary and excessive importance to the personality of the *messenger* and neglected the *Message*. This is the great error humanity has made in every age. In preferring the messenger to the Message, they preferred the pen to the letter. The letter and its author are important; the pen is only an instrument. Thus, differences came about in religion. The Message has been given in all periods;[20] when it was needed most, it was given loudly, when it was needed less, gently.

Jesus Christ said, "I am *alpha* and *omega*." (Rev. 1:11) This means that the messenger is 'first and last,' ever present.[21] The prophecy of Muhammad was this: now that all the world has received the Message through a human being, subject to all the limitations and conditions of human life, the Message will be given in the future without the claim.[22]

The Message is destined to reawaken the world, and to be a warning. The power of the force within is constantly at work, and this promises much for the core murids in the Sufi Order, to be the servant of a new era in the path of God and truth.

It is my wish that my murids who feel this trust in their hearts will not only receive this sacred Message for their own unfolding, but will feel the privilege of being a nucleus for the coming spiritual reconstruction of the world. The more conscious they are of this privilege, the more they will feel responsible for the duty they must perform. Murids show their devotion to the *murshid,* and to the cause, by doing their very best, and by devoting their thoughts and efforts in action to rebuilding the spiritual world.

The Sufi guards knowledge, wisdom, and power in humility. A Sufi does not dispute spiritual subjects with others. The spiritual evolution of each person differs from that of the other; the knowledge of one cannot be the knowledge of the other; nor is the understanding of one the understanding of the other. A Sufi does not discuss 'beliefs,' for the Sufi knows that at every step in spiritual evolution a person's belief changes until one arrives at a final belief which words cannot explain.

The Sufi learns not only by the study of books, but by the study of life. The whole of life is like an open book to a Sufi, and every experience is a step forward in one's spiritual journey.[23] A Sufi would rather learn than teach.[24] A Sufi begins life by discipline and resignation, realizing that the path that leads to the goal of freedom is the path of self-control, patience, resignation, and renunciation.

Freedom is the object of all esoteric schools, but you must not make the mistake of thinking that you can begin with that which is the end. To expect liberty in the beginning is to be like a seed thinking, 'I must be a tree at once and bear fruit.' The fruit is the outcome and object, the culmination of its existence. Freedom is the result of the journey. The path of freedom is an ideal; to understand the real meaning of it is not everyone's work.

The Sufi's method consists of this: the Sufi unites with the innermost being. Your heart is the shrine of God, and your body God's temple. The Sufi considers every person not only a sister or brother, but one's very own self. At the same time, the Sufi does not claim 'spirituality' or 'goodness'; nor do they judge others, only themselves in their own doings. The Sufi's attitude toward others is that of constant love and forgiveness. The Sufi's attitude toward God is that one's innermost being is the object of one's worship, the beloved whom one loves and admires.[25] The Sufi's interest in life is art and beauty, and one's task, the service of humanity in whatever form possible.

Notes on Gatheka V

1. Sufism is the old school of quietism . . .

In the 19th and early 20th centuries, many mystical movements were described as 'quietist,' referring to the "state of imperturbable serenity" observed among the adherents of such movements. According to the philosopher Arthur Schopenhauer, quietism is a doctrine of selflessness leading to deliverance from suffering.

2. As the origin of all the occult and mystical schools is the ancient school of Egypt . . .

An old tradition assumed from the Greeks and Romans.

3. From Sufism came four schools.

The four schools of Sufism were those of the Chishti, Naqshbandi, Qadiri, and Suhrawardi lineages. The four schools began their unification with the Chishti master, Shaykh Mahmud Rajan (d. 1495), who also carried the Suhrawardi transmission, and was continued by Shaykh Hasan Muhammad (d. 1575), who carried the Qadiri transmission, until finally being unified by Shah Kalim Allah Jahanabadi (1650-1729), as a carrier of the Naqshbandi transmission. Thus, it was a characteristic of masters within the Chishti-Nizami-Kalimi lineage, such as Inayat Khan, to emphasize training in the teachings and practices of all four schools.

4. "Be you perfect as your heavenly parent is perfect." (Matt. 5:48)

This mirrors the verse from Leviticus 20:7-8, "You are to hallow yourselves *(kadash),* to be holy *(kadosh),* for I, *Y-H-V-H,* am your God [and Holy]. You are to keep my laws and observe them; I, *Y-H-V-H,* am the one who hallows you *(kadash)!*" Also see Numbers 15:40 and Deuteronomy 26:18-19.

5. The Sufi Order represents the embodiment of all the schools and answers the need of the present day.

"Order" is a translation of the Arabic word, *tariqah*, meaning, 'way' or 'path,' and Sufi lineages are usually called *turuq*, 'paths' or 'orders.' When Inayat Khan founded The Sufi Order in London in 1918, there were no other Sufi orders active in Western Europe or North America. Being a master of the Chishti-Nizami-Kalimi lineage of "Four-School Sufism," uniting all the great lineages of Sufism and their teachings, and taking Sufism to its broadest universalistic conclusions, it made sense for Inayat Khan to speak of *"the* Sufi Order." However, today, with many Sufi lineages present in Western Europe and North America, we no longer refer to this lineage as "The Sufi Order."

In 2004, the Inayati-Maimuni lineage began to use the designation "Inayati" to publically distinguish the universalist Sufi lineage of Inayat Khan, as it is traditional in Sufism to use the name of a founder or place of origin to name a lineage. In 2016, the hereditary lineage of Pir Vilayat Inayat Khan and Pir Zia Inayat-Khan operating under the name, The Sufi Order, officially changed its name to The Inayati Order. Currently, all seven member organizations of the Federation of the Message identify as *Inayati* lineages, even if not in their official name.

6. The Sufi Order, therefore, is the body composed of those interested in spiritual attainment, initiated in the order formed in 1910, when the Sufi Message was brought to the Western world.

On September 13th, 1910, Inayat Khan departed from India at the direction of his *murshid* to come to the West. This is known as Hejirat Day among Inayati Sufis.

7. The Sufi path has Three Objects and Ten Thoughts.

The version of the "objects" and "thoughts" used in the Inayati-Maimuni Order differs slightly in form (rather than content) from those used by other Inayati Sufis. We generally speak of the "Ten Remembrances."

8. The rights of initiates in the Sufi Order are the same all over the world.

For our purposes, this is an acknowledgment of our common initiatic transmission.

9. *As an outer body, it has its* khanqah *and its branches.*

Khanqah is a Farsi (also, *khaneghah*) word for a building dedicated to Sufi practices, or a hospice for Sufi travelers.

10. *There are four circles of initiates: the study circle, the advanced circle, the inner circle, and the higher circle.*

In the Inayati-Maimuni Order, these are designated by the *maqamat* or 'stations' of the *murid, salik, faqir,* and *khalif.*

11. *When one is designated a 'Sufi,' the obligation to the group is finished.*

This is to suggest that the mature Sufi is fully individuated. And yet, contextually, in this passage, "Sufi" is used in two senses. The first sense is traditional. To speak of a true "Sufi" is to refer to someone of the highest attainment on the path. Thus, traditional Sufis often do not claim to be 'Sufis' at all, considering this the height of arrogance. On the other hand, the designation is practical, a name given to a group which aspires to such attainment. Inayat Khan—who was himself called "Sufi Inayat Khan"—uses this latter understanding to talk about more mature followers of the path.

12. *Then, if one wishes to continue to help humanity, one is authorized and initiated to work in that direction as a* khalif, *the 'deputy' of the guide, or as a* murshid, *the 'guide.'*

Murshid is Arabic for 'one who guides.' A *murshid* is the head of a circle of Sufis, a senior teacher or guide who has traversed the path and reached a clear integration of its elements. Another title for this role is *shaykh* (Arabic, lit. 'elder').

Khalif is Arabic for 'successor' or 'deputy.' A *khalif* is an heir and counselor to the *murshid*, one who is apprenticing in the art of spiritual guidance and acts as majordomo or master of ceremonies at Sufi gatherings. Even after one has become a *murshid*, one is still called a *khalif* of a particular *murshid*.

These roles are vocational and not steps on the path for everyone to tread. The goal of the Sufi is to become a *faqir*, a mature follower of the path. It is not to become a leader. That is a vocation and service chosen by God.

13. *Every initiated 'seeker' or* murid *is trusted with certain exercises or teachings.*

Murid is Arabic for 'one who seeks.' A *talib*, or 'candidate' for initiation, who truly becomes receptive to guidance is recognized as a *murid* by initiation. The *murid* forms a strong bond *(rabita)* with the *murshid*, 'the one who guides,' and follows the murshid's instructions diligently, according to Sheikh Mehmet Selim, "softening and opening the heart, undergoing tests of loyalty, continuing to question with utter politeness and sincerity, and (above all) fanning the flame of inspiration or of ardent devotion *(ishq)* to God."

14. *The* murid *is expected to keep the vow of secrecy, and to keep these not only from non-initiates, but also from other initiates.*

This is a traditional admonishment to prevent murids from speaking carelessly to the uninitiated and unprepared about matters and practices which require preparation and guidance.

15. *An exercise is a prescription meant for a particular person, and that person cannot pass it on to another.*

Oral teachings may be applicable to many, but they are always specifically meant for those who are present. This is something to keep in mind when reading such teachings, including the *Gathekas*.

16. *The study of a certain philosophy is not enough; there must be sincerity behind it.*

Sincerity is the most important practice on the path.

17. *Jesus Christ called this "faith."*

Faith is a virtue attributed to Jesus Christ by implication, in that he demonstrated unwavering faith. (Heb. 12:22; 10:37-38) It is also suggested that we should put our trust in him. (Heb. 2:13)

18. *In the Qur'an, it is said, "We have sent our messengers to every part of the Earth, that they may not say they were not warned in time."*

This is suggested in a number of qur'anic verses. Surah 57:25, says: "Indeed, we sent our messengers with clear signs; we sent down with them the book and the balance that these people would uphold justice." Surah 17:15 says: "Whoever is guided, is guided for the benefit of their soul. Whoever errs, errs against it. No bearer of burdens will bear the burden of another. We would never punish until we sent a messenger." Other suggestions of this idea are found in Surahs 2:15, 40:70, 16:36, and 43:45.

19. *All traditions declare that a messenger is given to the world at the time of the world's need.*

This is especially clear in the Hindu Vaishnava tradition of avatars, incarnations of God manifesting in the world at specific times of need. "Messenger" in Arabic is *rasul*, and the "message" is *risala*.

20. *The Message has been given in all periods . . .*

This suggests that the Message was being given in his time, and is also being given now.

21. *Jesus Christ said, "I am* alpha *and* omega." *(Rev. 1:11) This means that the messenger is 'first and last,' ever present.*

Jesus Christ in the vision of John the Divine said, "I am Alpha and Omega, the first and the last." There is an implied distinction between Jesus and Christ.

22. *The prophecy of Muhammad was this: now that all the world has received the Message through a human being, subject to all the limitations and conditions of human life, the Message will be given in the future without the claim.*

He is referring to the "claim" to be a 'messenger' or a 'prophet.' For Inayat Khan, the prophet Muhammad, as a messenger in his time, established that the essential Message of the unity of all being could be given through a simple human vessel, limited and imperfect, and yet no less divine. This Message was so clearly given that it only need be reiterated and no messenger need ever claim to be a "messenger" again.

23. *The whole of life is like an open book to a Sufi, and every experience is a step forward in one's spiritual journey.*

See the third of the "Ten Thoughts," or Inayati-Maimuni "Ten Remembrances."

24. *A Sufi would rather learn than teach.*

This is an admonition.

25. *The Sufi's attitude toward God is that one's innermost being is the object of one's worship, the beloved whom one loves and admires.*

The traditional root metaphors for the relationship with God are as the 'Friend' and the 'Beloved.'

26. *The Sufi's interest in life is art and beauty, and one's task, the service of humanity in whatever form possible.*

As it says in the famous tradition of the prophet Muhammad, "God is beautiful and loves beauty." Thus, the Sufi sees art and beauty as gateways to God.

GATHEKA VI
The Intoxication of Life

There are many intoxicating things in life;[1] but if you consider the nature of life, you will find that there is nothing more intoxicating than life itself. Think of what you were yesterday and compare it with today; the unhappiness, happiness, riches or poverty of yesterday, are a dream; only your condition today matters.

This life of rising and falling, of continual change, is like running water. With the running of this water, we think, *'I am this water.'* In reality, we do not know what we are. If we go from poverty to riches, and then from riches to poverty, we mourn when those riches taken away again. We mourn because we have forgotten that we were poor before having those riches, and from that poverty we became rich.

If you consider your past desires, you will find that you had different desires at every stage of your development. At one time, you longed for a particular thing for which you could not have cared less at another. If you look at your life as a spectator, you will see that it is full of intoxication. What gives you pride and satisfaction at one moment, humiliates you at another. What you enjoy at one time, troubles you at another. What you value in one moment, you do not later.

Observe your actions in everyday life. If you have an awakened sense of justice and understanding,[2] you will admit to doing things you had not intended, or to saying something that you would not want to have said. We ask ourselves, 'Why was I such a fool?' Sometimes you seem to love someone, or admire them, and it persists for days, weeks, months, or even years. Then, one day, you suddenly feel, 'I was wrong,' or there comes along someone more attractive, and suddenly you are on another path. Suddenly, you do not know where you are, or who you love!

In the actions and reactions of life, sometimes you do things on impulse without considering what you are actually doing; and occasionally, a good impulse leads you to do what you actually think is right. Then, a certain reactivity takes over, and all those good intentions are suddenly gone. In business, in professions and commerce, on an impulse you might say, 'I must do this,' or 'I must do that,' and you seem to have all the strength and courage necessary to see your objective through. But often the resolve only lasts a day or two, and then you forget what you were doing, and you want to do something else.

Like a piece of driftwood, we are raised and cast down by the waves of the life. Thus, Hindus have called the life of the world, *bawasada*, an ocean. We are floating in this ocean of activity, unaware of what we are actually doing, unaware of where we are going. Only this moment called 'the present' is important; the past is a dream, the future is in a mist; the only thing clear is the present.

The attachment, the love and affection of a person in the world is sometimes not very different from the attachment of birds and animals. There is a time when the sparrow looks after its young, brings grains in its beak and puts them into the beaks of its young, who anxiously await the coming of their mother. This goes on until their wings are grown. Once the young have flown free in the forest under the protection of their gentle mother, knowing other branches of the tree, they never again see the mother who was once so kind to them. There are often moments of emotion, impulses of love, of attachment, of affection that pass away, becoming pale and faded. There comes a time when a person thinks that there is something else desirable, something else to like or love.[3]

The more you think of an adult's life in the world, the more you see that it is not very different from the life of a child. The child takes a fancy to a doll, then gets tired of the doll, taking a fancy to another toy. When the child takes a fancy to the doll or toy, they think it the most valuable thing in the world. Then comes a day when the child breaks the doll or destroys the toy.

So it is with each adult. Our scope is perhaps a little different, but our actions are the same. All that we consider important in life—the collection of wealth, the possession of property, the attainment of fame, and rising to a position that we think ideal—all of these objects have an intoxicating effect on us. But after attaining the object, we are not satisfied. We think, 'I want something else; this is not what I really wanted!' Whatever we want, we feel it is the most important thing in the world; but after attaining it, we think it is not that important and we want something else.

In everything that pleases us and makes us happy—our amusements, our theater, our moving pictures, golf, polo, tennis—it seems that it amuses us to be in a puzzle. It seems that we only want to fill our time; we do not actually want to know where we are going or what we are reeally doing. What a person calls 'pleasure' is the moment in which they are intoxicated with the activity of life.

Anything that covers our eyes from reality, anything that makes us feel sensation in life, anything we can indulge, is what we call 'pleasure.' Our nature is such that whatever we become accustomed to, that is our pleasure—eating, drinking, or almost any activity. If we become accustomed to something bitter, that bitterness is our pleasure; if sour, then sourness is our pleasure; if sweets, then sweets are our pleasure.

Once you get into the habit of complaining about your life, you begin to look for something about which to complain, even if there is nothing. Others want sympathy, to complain that they are badly treated, and so they look for some treatment about which to complain. *Intoxication.*

The thief has a habit of stealing; they are pleased by stealing and get into a habit of theft. If another path is offered them, they are displeased and do not want to take it. *Intoxication.*

There are many with whom it becomes a habit to worry. The least little thing worries them. They cherish the least concern and worry about it; it is a plant which they water and nourish.

Many, directly or indirectly, consciously or unconsciously, become accustomed to illness; the illness is sometimes more of an intoxication than a reality. As long as they hold the thought of that illness, they sustain it, and the illness settles into the body so that no doctor can take it away.

Sorrow can also be an intoxication.

Every circumstance, every individual environment, and every condition in life, creates an illusion and intoxicates us, so that we cannot see the real need and circumstances of the people around us, the people of the cities in which we live, the countries in which we dwell. This intoxication is with us in our waking life through the day, and even continues in our dreams, as a drunk will often dream of things that have to do with drunkenness. If you have joy, if you have sorrow, if you have a worry, or if you have a pleasure, the same will manifest in your dreams. Day and night, the dream continues; the dream lasts a lifetime with some, and with others only a season.

People love their intoxication as much as the drunk loves wine. When a person finds something interesting in their dreams, and somebody else tries to wake them, even on waking, they feel they should go back to sleep and finish the dream. Knowing it was a dream, they still wish to finish it. This intoxication is seen in all aspects of life; it manifests even in the religious, philosophical, and mystical aspects of life.

People most want to know what they cannot understand; they are pleased to be told something that their reason cannot understand. Give someone the simple truth and they will not like it. When teachers like Jesus Christ came and gave the Message of truth in simple words, the people said, 'This is in our book; we know it already!' But when people attempt to mystify others, talking of fairies, ghosts, and spirits, people are pleased; they want to understand what they cannot understand.

What has been called 'spiritual' or 'religious truth' is the key to that ultimate truth which we cannot see because of our intoxication. No one can give this truth to anyone else. It is in every soul; the human soul is itself this truth. What we give with regard to this truth is the means by which it can be known. The religions, in different forms, have been *methods*. By these methods, people have been taught by inspired souls to know this truth, which is in the soul of each person, and to be benefited by it. But many others have taken only the external part of the religion and forgotten the truth, fighting wars with one another, declaring, 'My religion is true, and yours is false.'

Nevertheless, there have always existed the wise, like those of the East who came to see the Christ child when he was born.[4] What does that mean? It means that, at different times, those whose life's mission has been to keep themselves sober—the wise—have existed, in spite of the intoxication all around them, to help their fellow human beings gain their own sobriety. Among the wise by sobriety, there have been some of great inspiration, great power and control over themselves, over life within and without. It is such people who have been called saints or sages, prophets or masters.

Even those who have followed and accepted the wise, have monopolized them in their intoxication, fighting with others in their drunkenness, calling their own prophet or teacher the only prophet or teacher. And just as a drunk would, without thinking, hit or hurt another person who might be different from them, who thought, felt, or did something differently, so the great ones who have come to help humanity have often been killed, crucified, hurt, or tortured. They have not complained, however; they have taken it as a natural consequence of their work. They have understood that they were in a world of intoxication, and that it is natural that a drunk will hurt or harm others. That has been the history in whatever part of the world the Message of God has been given.

In reality, the Message has one source, and that is God. Whatever name the wise have given that Message, it was not *their* Message; it was the Message of God. Those whose hearts had eyes to see and ears to hear have known and seen the same messenger, because they have received the Message. Those whose hearts have no eyes or ears have thought the messenger most important and neglected the Message. In whatever period that Message arrived, and in whatever form it was garbed, there was only one Message, the Message of wisdom.[5]

The drunkenness of the world has increased to such an extent that great bloodshed and disaster have come about recently, the like of which cannot be found in the history of the world.[6] This shows us that the world's drunkenness has reached its summit. No one can deny that even now the world is not sober. Even now the traces of that drunkenness can be found in the unrest of our time, even if the great bloodshed is over for the moment.

Sufism is connected to the word *sophia*, meaning 'wisdom.' It is the Message of wisdom. Its aim has been the same in all periods of the world's history. The aim of the Message is to bring sobriety to humanity, to bring about love for one's neighbor. No doubt, politics, education, and business are a means of bringing people of different races and nations into contact with one another; but spiritual truth and the understanding of life is the only means of bringing about the feeling of fellowship in the world.

GATHEKA VI

This Message does not form an exclusive community. There are already many such communities fighting against one another. The object of the Message is to bring about a better understanding between different communities in the knowledge of truth. This is not a new religion. How can this be a new religion when Jesus Christ has said, "I have not come to give a new law; I have come to fulfill religion."[7] (Matt. 5:17-18) This is the combination of the religions.[8]

The chief aim of this Sufi Movement is to revive the religions of the world, and bring the followers of different religions together in friendly understanding and tolerance. All are received with open arms among Sufis. Whatever their religion, to whatever house of worship they belong, there is no interference with it. There is personal help and guidance in the methods of meditation. There is a course of study to consider the problems of life.[9] The chief aim of every Sufi is to do their best to bring about such understanding, so that all of humanity may become one single family in the parenthood of God.

Notes on Gatheka VI

1. *There are many intoxicating things in life . . .*

Intoxicating substances are discouraged and even forbidden in most expressions of Islam, thus, the concept and discussion of 'intoxication' became very important in the historical development of Sufism.

2. *Observe your actions in everyday life. If you have an awakened sense of justice and understanding . . .*

Note that "an awakened sense of justice" is similar to the fifth of the "Ten Thoughts" or Inayati-Maimuni "Ten Remembrances."

3. *There comes a time when a person thinks that there is something else desirable, something else to like or love.*

As human beings, we must not only honor the *feeling* of falling in love, or feeling *in love* in a particular moment, but also the *investment* of love, and then the *re-investment* in love throughout our lives.

4. *Nevertheless, there have always existed the wise, like those of the East who came to see the Christ child when he was born.*

This episode is found in the Gospels, Matthew chapter 2. For Inayat Khan, it was certainly significant that they were called, *'magi,'* a name connected with Zoroastrianism.

5. *In whatever period that Message arrived, and in whatever form it was garbed, there was only one Message, the Message of wisdom.*

The teaching that the Message *(risala)* was offered to humanity at different times through different vehicles is a legitimate part of all three Abrahamic traditions.

6. *The drunkenness of the world has increased to such an extent that great bloodshed and disaster have come about recently, the like of which cannot be found in the history of the world.*

This is a reference to World War I, which taught us a new scale upon which war could be fought, and also that wars do not need religions as causes. World War I is remembered as a completely senseless personal conflict with needless loss of life.

7. *How can this be a new religion when Jesus Christ has said, "I have not come to give a new law; I have come to fulfill religion."*

This is a paraphrase of two consecutive verses from the Gospels, Matthew 5:17-18.

8. *This is the combination of the religions.*

It is possible that Inayat Khan is suggesting what we are seeing today, the fusing of religions in new ways, new combinations, building a larger unified perspective. Of course, this has always been true.

GATHEKA VI

9. *There is personal help and guidance in the methods of meditation. There is a course of study to consider the problems of life.*

This suggests that the Sufi path is first and foremost a school of experiential study and practice.

10. *The chief aim of every Sufi is to do their best to bring about such understanding, that all of humanity may become one single family in the parenthood of God.*

"One single family in the Parenthood of God" is similar to the sixth of the "Ten Thoughts" or Inayati-Maimuni "Ten Remembrances."

GATHEKA VII
THE PATH OF INITIATION

In the true sense of the word 'initiation,' the word itself is its meaning. Initiation means taking initiative in a direction not generally understood by others. Therefore, initiation requires courage and the tendency to advance spiritually. Therefore, the first duty of a *murid* is not to be shaken by opposition, or anything said against the path they have taken. You must not allow yourself to be discouraged. A *murid* must be so firm, that even if the whole world says, 'It is wrong,' the *murid* maintains, 'It is right for me.' If someone says it will take a thousand years, a *murid* must be able to say, 'If it takes a thousand years, I must be patient.'

In Persian, it is the work of the *baz*, the wayfarer of the heavens.[1] In the mystical path, courage, steadiness, and patience are the most necessary attributes, as well as trust in the teacher whose hand has been taken in initiation,[2] and an understanding of discipline. In the East, where for thousands of years the path of discipleship has been understood, these things are regarded as extremely important and acceptable from the hand of the teacher, at least to the extent the *murid* understands discipline and trusts in the teacher.

Few people in the world really know trust! What is necessary is not trusting another, or even the teacher, but trusting oneself. But those who have not experienced trust of another are not capable of fully trusting themselves.

What if our trust is broken? Should we not be disappointed? The answer is, we must trust for the sake of trusting, not for the sake of return or what it might bring. It is ultimate trust that is the greatest power in the world. Lack of trust is a weakness. Even if you lose by trust, your power is greater than if you have gained without developing trust.

Patience is also necessary on the path. It may surprise you, but it was six months after my initiation into the order of the Sufis, and being continually in the presence of my *murshid*, that he first said a word on the subject of Sufism. It will amuse you even more to know that as soon as I took out my notebook he went on to another subject! One sentence after six months! You might think, 'What a long time to wait—six months sitting before your teacher and nothing taught!' But friends, it is not about words; it is something else. If words were sufficient, there are libraries full of books of mystical and occult ideas. It is *life* itself; it is in the *living.* Those who live the life of initiation are actually *alive* and make others who come into contact with them *alive,* too. Remember, therefore, that in Sufism you are initiated not only for study, but also to understand and follow the ways of real discipleship.

As for discipline, to be without discipline is to be without self-control. It is discipline that teaches the ideal, and the ideal is self-discipline. It is the soldier who can become a good captain. In ancient times, kings made their princes learn to be soldiers in order to learn what discipline meant. The path of initiation is the training of the ego; it is self-discipline that is learned in the way of discipleship.

What is the path of initiation? What should our goal be? What must we expect from it? Should we expect to be good, healthy, magnetic, powerful, physically developed, or clairvoyant? No. You will cultivate all these things naturally; but do not strive for these things. Suppose you develop power and do not know its proper use; the outcome will be disastrous.

GATHEKA VII

Suppose you develop magnetism, and attract all—good and bad. It will be difficult to get rid of what you have attracted. Or imagine you are very good, so good that everyone is bad to you, too good to live in the world; you will become a burden to yourself. These things are not to be sought in initiation.

The aim is to find God within yourself, to dive so deep within that you may touch the unity of all being. Through initiation, you work toward this end, so that from within you may find inspiration and blessing in your life.

For that, two things are necessary: one is to do the exercises that are given to you, regularly, and with heart; the second is that the studies which are assigned to you should not be considered 'just a little reading.' No, every word should be pondered. The more you think on it, the more it will have the effect of opening the heart. Reading is one thing, contemplating is another. The *Gathas* must be contemplated.[3] Do not take even the simplest word or sentence as 'simple.' Consider the Hindus, the Chinese, and the Parsis who, for more than a millennium, have contemplated their sacred writings and never tired of them.

Notes on Gatheka VII

1. *In Persian, it is the work of the* baz, *the wayfarer of the heavens.*

   Baz is Arabic and Farsi for 'falcon.'

2. *In the mystical path, courage, steadiness, and patience are the most necessary attributes, as well as trust in the teacher whose hand has been taken in initiation . . .*

   During *bay'ah,* 'initiation' into a Sufi lineage, one takes the right hand of the *murshid. Bay'ah* is literally a 'pledge' of allegiance. Initiation is also commonly called, 'taking hand.'

3. *The* Gathas *must be contemplated.*

   The *Gathas* are a group of teachings of Inayat Khan to be studied by murids of the order.

GATHEKA VIII
Reincarnation

People have often asked me, 'What does the Sufi say about reincarnation?' Sometimes I have answered them with silence; sometimes I have answered positively, sometimes negatively. Some may have thought that I did not believe in it, and if *I* did not believe in it, then no Sufis believed in it. But this is not the case. Every Sufi is free to believe whatever they consider to be right, or whatever they can understand. A Sufi is not nailed down to any particular belief. By believing in a doctrine, a Sufi does not cease to be a Sufi; nor does disbelief force them from Sufism. There is perfect freedom of belief.

There was a reason for my positive response to the question of reincarnation, just as there was a reason for my negative response. The reason did not have as much to do with me as with the person who asked the question. People wish to make things rigid, things of the subtlest nature, which words cannot explain. When a person describes the 'hereafter,' it is like wanting to weigh the soul or photograph the spirit. Personally, I think you have to realize what the hereafter is for yourself. You must not depend upon my words alone. Self-realization is the aim. Beliefs in doctrines are like pills given to the sick to address various problems.

All things are true to a certain extent, but fall short of proving themselves existent when compared with the ultimate truth. Things appear differently from different angles. When a person on the ground asks a person standing on a mountain,

'What do you believe?' What can the person on the mountain convey to the person on the ground? The questioner must climb the mountain and see for themselves. Until then, there is no genuine understanding between them, no matter the quality of the description.

The method of the Sufi is stillness and contemplation, allowing one to see for themselves in time. The spiritual path is for the patient, and patience is extremely difficult.

Notes on Gatheka VII

1. *People have often asked me, 'What does the Sufi say about reincarnation?'*

This was a major preoccupation of Inayat Khan's early audiences, often comprised of people who had read theosophical literature or attended theosophical circles, or people who had some exposure to the Vedanta Society.

2. *All things are true to a certain extent, but fall short of proving themselves existent when compared with the ultimate truth.*

Non-dual philosophies make a distinction between relative and absolute truth.

GATHEKA IX
Impressions Within and Without

Interdependence can be considered from various points of view. Consider how all of which we partake—food, drink, medicine—impact our physical body. Heavier food, lighter food, purer food, all manifest outwardly. The body has inherited its nature from the earth to which it belongs. The nature of earth is such that when it takes the seed of flowers, it produces flowers; when it receives the seed of fruit, it produces fruit; and when it is poisoned, it poisons. What it takes in becomes the result. There is nothing you ingest, eat, or drink, that will not manifest in the body. Moreover, the body also acts upon the mind, as the mind acts upon the body. Consider how intoxicants impact the mind. Something material, which is taken into the body, can affect the mind, which is not material.

The mind is far greater than scientists now consider it, thinking it identical with the brain. In Sanskrit, the word for 'mind' is *mana*, from which we get the English words 'mind' and 'man.'[1]

What is a human being, really? What is one's mind? In the teachings of Jesus Christ, a person is as one thinks; a person is their thought; a person is their mind.[2] We attribute so much of our identity to our bodies, but our true identity is with our minds.

All that of which we partake, mentally or physically, has an affect on the mind. If we partake of foods or intoxicants, they not only affect the body, but the mind as well. That of which the mind partakes through the senses has an influence upon the body. For instance, all that one sees is impressed upon the mind. There is no help for it; it is an automatic process; the impression is simply recorded there. All that one hears, smells, tastes, or touches, impacts the mind as well as the body. Our contact with the outer world is such that there is a continual interchange; every moment of our lives we partake of all that which our senses partake.

Even those who are looking for faults in others, or looking at evil—though not themselves wicked—often partake of evil without knowing it. For instance, the impression made on our consciousness by a deceitful person lingers and influences us, even as we cast our gaze on an honest person, causing us to question their honesty. This is how a pessimistic attitude is born.

A person once deceived is always on the lookout for deceit. They will look for deceit even in the honest owing to that impression. A hunter, once attacked by a lion in the forest, may be frightened when touched by their own gentle mother because of the remaining impression of the lion.

Consider all the impressions, agreeable and disagreeable, we acquire from morning till evening without knowing the consequences. In this way, we may become wicked without any intention to be so.

No one is born wicked. Although the body belongs to the earth, the soul belongs to God. From above, we have received nothing but goodness. The wickedest person in the world is nothing but goodness in the deepest depth of their being. If there is any such thing as 'wickedness' or 'badness' in someone, it has been acquired naturally, as everyone is open to impressions.

The secret of what may be called 'superstition' or an 'omen' is in the impression. For instance, some believe that if you hear the sound of a certain bell, there will be a death in your surroundings, or if you see a particular person, good or bad luck will befall your family. People have sometimes believed such things blindly, and gone on believing them for many years. Intellectuals often believe there is nothing to these superstitions and ignore them. But, after careful study, one will find that the secret of all those superstitions is nothing but the impression; whatever the mind has taken in through the senses has its effect, not only upon the body, but also upon one's life.

Over time, the physical features of our faces can take on the characteristics of the impressions made upon our minds. It is written in the Qur'an that every part of our being bears witness to our actions.[3] I would suggest that the effect of this 'witness' is not only in the hereafter, but made upon every hour of the day. If you examine life closely, you will find that the mind and body are formed from what one takes from the outer world.

In the words of Christ, "Where your treasure is, there will be your heart, also." (Matt. 6:21) All that we value is what we make in ourselves; we create all that we value. An admirer of beauty will always partake of all that they believe beautiful, whether of form, color, line, or of manner and attitude, which are greater still.

As the world is today, people ignore much of the beauty of real culture and refinement. It is a warning that the world is sliding backward. Civilization is not only about industrial development or material culture. If that is 'civilization,' it is not the right word. Civilization is progress toward love, harmony, and beauty. When one abandons these three great principles, one may still be creative, but it will not create civilization.

Every culture and people have their ideas of right and wrong; but there is one fundamental principle in which all religions, all cultures and people can meet; that is the principle of seeing beauty in action, attitude, thought, and feeling. There is no action upon which there is a universal stamp which says, 'this is wrong' or 'right' What is wrong or wicked is what our mind is accustomed to seeing as 'wrong' or 'wicked' because it is devoid of love, harmony, and beauty.

Those who truly seek beauty in all its forms—in action, manner, and feeling—will stamp their hearts with beauty. All the great beings who have come into the world, awakening humanity to a greater truth, have brought us *beauty*. It is not what they taught; it is what they were in themselves.

The intellectual understanding of beauty, mere 'talk of beauty,' is not enough. Words are inadequate to express beauty and goodness. One can speak a thousand thoughts and never express it. It is beyond words. The soul alone understands it.

Those who always follow the rule of beauty in life, in every thing they do, will always succeed; they will always be able to discriminate between right and wrong, between good and bad.

Notes on Gatheka IX

1. *In Sanskrit, the word for 'mind' is* mana, *from which we get the English words 'mind' and 'man.'*

Sanskrit and English are both from the Indo-European language group, thus *mana* and man both come from the Indo-European root, *manu-*, meaning 'mind.'

2. *In the teachings of Jesus Christ, a person is as one thinks; a person is their thought; a person is their mind.*

This is probably based on statements such as those found in Matthew 5:27-28.

3. *It is written in the Qur'an that every part of our being bears witness to our actions.*

This may be a reference to Surah 75.

GATHEKA X
The Truth and the Way

Looking at the subject from a spiritual point of view, the idea of religion is illustrated by a story told in India of Aladdin and the magic lantern.[1] What is the magic lantern? It is hidden in the heart of every soul. Its light is covered over time, and from this the whole tragedy of life arises. Why do we seek happiness? It is not because we love happiness or would like to be happy. We seek for it because we are unaware that we *are* happiness. The mistake we make is in seeking happiness outside ourselves instead of within.

The most powerful words spoken by Christ were, "I am the truth and I am the way."[2] Think about that. These are two things—"the truth" and "the way." When people confuse these two things they become perplexed and cannot find "the way." Too often we use the word 'truth' when discussing facts; but truth is something that uproots or overturns facts. What then is 'fact'? Fact is the illusion of truth; it is not the truth.

Now, what is truth? That is the one thing you cannot speak of in words. During my travels, people have often asked me to tell them something about 'the truth.' I have been asked this so often that I want to write 'truth' on a brick and hand it to them, saying, 'Now hold on to this; this is the truth.' If truth were so small that words could contain it, then it would not be the truth.

Sufis have always used the Arabic word for 'truth'—*Haqq*—which means 'God-self.' That is the truth we are all seeking.

It is so interesting to see that, however dishonest a person may be, they do not want anyone else to deceive them. A person whose profession may involve lying from morning till evening still does not want their spouse to lie to them when they come home.

We are contented with facts, supposing they are truth. By this contentment, so many in this world fight with one another. But nothing can satisfy the craving of the soul which is continually in search of that truth which no words can utter.

"I am the way" is a great problem to consider. The one who wants to find "the way" often makes a mistake. One may find it, but it is not always easy. It is strange that people give years and years to the study of grammar, music, or science, but when it comes to the truth, they want a simple answer. If it were merely a lack of patience, that would be excusable; but often it is simply that they rarely consider the truth.

If one is eager or impatient, one might possibly reach the truth in one step; at least there is every reason to be hopeful. It is difficult to find gold; it is less difficult to find the truth. Gold is hidden outside ourselves; but truth is something within us. People search all their lives for something that can only be found within.

The reason is not because there is not already "a way" between us and God. There is a way between each one of us and God; but we have gone astray. Therefore, each of us is shown "the way" by an elder sister or brother. That way is available to birds and insects and all creatures. God is the perfection of justice, and God has not excluded any soul, however small, from this bliss.

It seems that even the birds and beasts concentrate. They meditate in their own way and offer their prayers to God. There is no being on Earth, however small, which does not contemplate. If your sight were keen enough, sitting in the solitary woods or in a mountain cave, you would see that all creatures have their prayers and their *at-one-ment* with God. Why do the great—those souls who find no rest and peace in the world—go to the wilderness? To breathe the breath of peace and calm that comes in the heart of the wilderness.

Human beings—the most intelligent of all creatures—have gone the most astray. We have created an artificial world as an improvement upon nature; but in creating it, we have lost our way. Are we happy in this 'paradise' we have made?[3] Do we not cause more and more bloodshed? Are we not unjust to our fellow beings? How can a world of intoxication, absorbing all of our mind, time, and effort, give us that happiness which our soul is craving?

From time to time, "the way" is shown to those who lift their gaze from this world and ask for guidance. Although "the way" seems far, the distance cannot be compared with the distances of this Earth.

The way is so short—less than an inch—and yet can be as long and as distant as thousands of worlds. "The way" contracts and stretches according to the attitude of the soul. However, there is one hope: "The one who comes to me but one step, I go forward to them one hundred steps."[4]

There are many different opinions about how the condition of this world should be bettered: some think by religious reform; some think by educational reform; and some think by social reform. Every reform made with the idea of doing some good is worthwhile. But the reform most needed is spiritual reform. The hour has come when narrowness of perspective must be abandoned in order to rise above those differences and distinctions which divide human beings. Rising will raise our neighbors. The sustainer of all is not pleased when some of God's children are considered sisters and brothers, and others are not. No mother or father is pleased at seeing some children favored and others neglected. We need to train ourselves to love one another.

By spiritual reform, I do not mean 'wonder-working' or talking about metaphysical problems. The problem to be solved is solved by itself. We have only to wish and it is solved. The problem we have to solve is the problem of reconciliation and reconstruction, which politicians have not been able to solve, because it can only be solved by a spiritual awakening.

The way to spirituality is the expansion and widening of the heart. In order to accommodate the divine truth, the heart must be expanded. With the expansion of the heart, the divine bliss is poured forth.

True spirituality is raising consciousness to the abode of divine being.

Notes on Gatheka X

1. *Looking at the subject from a spiritual point of view, the idea of religion is illustrated by a story told in India of Aladdin and the magic lantern.*

This tale is given in the extended collections of the *Arabian Nights;* it is actually a popular addition to the original collection.

2. *The most powerful words spoken by Christ were, "I am the truth and I am the way."*

This is a paraphrase from the Gospels, John 14:6: "I am the way and the truth and the life."

3. *Are we happy in this 'paradise' we have made?*

The original meaning of "paradise" was 'an enclosed garden.'

4. *"The one who comes to me but one step, I go forward to them one hundred steps."*

This may be a version of a *hadith qudsi* such as the one found in *Sahih al-Bukhari* 97:34: "If you come a span nearer to Me, I will come a cubit nearer to you; and if you come a cubit nearer to Me, I will come a distance of two outstretched arms nearer to you; and if you come to Me walking, I go to you running."

GATHEKA XI

SUFI MYSTICISM I

The Mystic's Path in Life

There is one God, one truth, one religion, one mysticism, whether it is called Sufism, Christianity, Hinduism, or Buddhism. As God cannot be divided, neither can mysticism. It is an error to say, 'My religion is different from yours.' That is a misunderstanding of religion. There cannot be more than one mysticism, just as there cannot be more than one wisdom. There is only one wisdom. It is an error to say, 'This is Eastern; that is Western.' This shows a lack of wisdom. All peoples have the divine truth, no matter where they come from in the world.

It is an error to say, 'This is my eye, and that is yours.' The two eyes belong to one being. When a person pictures mysticism as a branch of a tree which is truth, they are wrong, for mysticism is the trunk which unites all the branches.

What is mysticism, really? Mysticism is the way to realize the truth. Jesus Christ said, "I am the way and the truth." (John 14:6) He did not say, "I am the *ways* and the *truths*," for there is only one way. If there is another, it is the wrong way. There are many religions; but not many wisdoms. There are many houses for worship; but only one God. There are many scriptures; but only one truth. There are many methods; but not many ways. It is either the right way or the wrong way.

The methods of gaining this *way* of realization are many, but may be reduced to four—by the heart, by the head, by action, and by repose.[1] We choose among these four methods of developing ourselves and preparing to journey on the way— the only way—called mysticism. No religion can call it its own; it is the way of all religions. No sect can say that it belongs to it; it belongs to all sects. No person can say that the way they have chosen is *the* way. All get there by the same way.

People often imagine that a mystic is an ascetic, a hermit, or an impractical dreamer who dwells in the air and does not live here on earth. But this is not true. Often people want to see the mystic as a peculiar sort of person, as an eccentric. If someone is peculiar in a certain way, they call them 'a mystic.' This is a misconception and a one-sided exaggeration. The real mystic must demonstrate equilibrium and balance. The head of the real mystic touches the heavens while their feet are on the ground.

The real mystic is as wide-awake in *this* world as in the other. A mystic is not without intellect; a mystic is not a dreamer. A mystic is wide-awake, and yet capable of dreaming when others are not, capable of keeping awake when others cannot. A mystic strikes the balance between power and beauty. A mystic does not sacrifice power for beauty, nor beauty for power. A mystic possesses power and enjoys beauty.

As to the life of the mystic, there is balance, reason, love, and harmony. The religion of the mystic is every religion, all religions, and yet the mystic is above what people call their religion. In point of fact, the mystic *is* religion. The moral of all religion is reciprocity: to reciprocate all the kindness we receive, to do an act of kindness without expecting appreciation or a return of kindness, and to make every sacrifice, however great, for love, harmony and beauty.

The God of the mystic is found in the heart. The truth of the mystic is beyond words. People argue and debate about things of little importance; but mysticism is not to be discussed. People talk in order to know something and then forget everything.

Often it is not the one who knows a lot who talks a lot, but the one who wants to know. The mystic knows that happiness is in the heart. Putting it into words is like trying to put the ocean into a drop.

The mystic drinks the wine of ecstasy. This wine is so powerful that the intoxicated mystic's presence becomes a wine for everyone who meets them. This wine is the wine of the true sacrament, the symbol of which is in the church.

What is it? Where does it come from? What is it made of? You may call it power, life, strength, which comes through the mystic, through spheres to which everyone is attached. Through their attachment to these spheres, the mystic drinks the sustaining wine of the human soul, the wine of ecstasy, the mystic's intoxication. That intoxication is the love that manifests in the human heart. Once the mystic drinks that wine, what does it matter if they are sitting on the rocks in the wilderness or in a palace? It is all the same. The palace does not increase the pleasure of the mystic, nor does the rock take it away. The mystic has found the sovereignty of God on Earth, about which Jesus Christ has said, "Seek you first the kingdom of God and all these things will be added unto you." (Luke 12:31)

People strive for many different things in this world, but only seek the spiritual path after everything else. Some are indifferent, saying, 'There is a long life before me; when the time comes that I must awake, I'll awaken.' But the mystic says, 'Waking is the one thing I have to do—all other things come after.' It is the most important thing in the mystic's life.

Should the mystic, in working for realization of God, neglect their duties in the world? This is not necessary. There is nothing that a mystic should renounce in order to have the realization of life. It is only necessary to give the greatest importance to what is of the greatest importance in life. Ordinary people give it the least importance; the mystic gives it the first importance.

You might ask, 'Is the life of a mystic meditative?' Yes, but meditation for a mystic is like the winding of a clock. It is wound and then runs by itself all day. The mystic does not have to think about it, or worry about it, for the rest of the day. There was a *shah* of Persia who used to stay up for long night vigils and prayers.[2] A visitor wondered at his meditating after a long day's work. "It is too much," they said. "You do not need meditation." "Do not say so," said the *shah*. "You do not know what you are saying. At night, I pursue God; during the day, God pursues me."

Your moments of meditation set the whole mechanism running, like a stream running into the ocean. It does not take the mystic away from their duty in the least; it blesses every word they speak with the thought of God.

In all the mystic thinks, in all the mystic does, is the healing and blessing perfume of God.

How does the mystic, who has become kind and helpful, get along amid the rough crowd of everyday life? The rough edges of everyday life wear on the mystic and make the mystic's heart-sore, more sore than the hearts of others. The kind and patient take all the thorns. Like the cut and faceted diamond, the cut and faceted heart becomes brilliant. The heart, sufficiently cut, becomes a flame that illuminates the life of the mystic, and the lives of others.

Notes on Gatheka XI

1. *The methods of gaining this way of realization are many, but may be reduced to four—by the heart, by the head, by action, and by repose.*

These four correspond to the Four Yogas of the Vedanta tradition— Bhakti Yoga (discipline of devotion), Jnana Yoga (discipline of intellect), Karma Yoga (discipline of action), and Raja Yoga (discipline of meditation).

GATHEKA XI

2. *There was a* shah *of Persia who used to stay up for long night vigils and prayers.*

    Shah is a Persian (Farsi) term for a 'monarch.'

GATHEKA XII
SELF-REALIZATION
Awakening the Inner Senses

Why do we study? Is it for the acquisition of spiritual powers or phenomena, for inspirations or curiosity? All these reasons are wrong. Is it for the accomplishment of something material or for worldly success? This is not desirable.

Self-realization—to know *what* we are—should be our aim.

Some people who admire piety and goodness want everyone to be angels. When they discover this is impossible, they become critical. Everyone has a 'devil' in them, and everyone has an 'angel.' Everyone is at once human and animal.[1] It is the 'devil' in us that drives us to do harm, seemingly without a motive, as if by instinct. The first step should be to abandon this attitude. No one believes that their own particular 'demon' can be a manifestation of the devil. But who can really say, 'I am free from the influence of such a negative spirit?' We can all come under the power of spells, and we must overcome such power. Everyone can fight this. We must liberate ourselves from negativity.

We must discover when we have manifested or are manifesting our 'devil' or animal nature. What we want to manifest is a human spirit. Self-realization is the search for this human spirit. Everything must become human in us. But how do we accomplish this? Do we read the Bible or other holy scriptures? All these books tell us what we should do; but we must also find the store of goodness in our hearts. As you cultivate the heart, it rises. Through ascetic practices, you can develop the soul and reach ecstasy; but of what use is *samadhi* or meditative absorption if we are not first, human? If we want to live in this world, we must be human; the ascetic should live in a forest.

How should we cultivate the heart? No doubt, harmlessness, devotion, and kindness are necessary; but there is something else. There is a center which, when awakened, makes one sensitive, not only externally, but also mentally.

There are two kinds of people: one is struck by the beauty of music or other manifestations of beauty, and the other is dull as a stone to these.

Why? Because something in their heart and mind is not awakened. We have five senses; but we also have inner senses, and these can enjoy life more keenly.

Some will say, 'I need no inner senses; my outer senses satisfy me completely.' They would speak differently if, for instance, they lost an eye or another of their five senses. In order to be complete, a human being must develop the inner senses, also. But first, one should develop one's inner feeling.

There is no end to intellectual study. For this reason, the spiritual teacher does not encourage speculation. A doctrine is separate from other doctrines; but the Sufi belongs to every religion. The Sufi has no special beliefs or speculations. There can, for instance, be one Sufi who believes in reincarnation and another who realizes heaven and hell. The work of the Sufi is personal development. What you practice is more important than what the teacher says. The teacher can give you protection. The teacher can say, 'Yes, it's true; that is my experience also.'

Initiation has several degrees. The teacher offers trust, but the real initiation is the work of God. No teacher can judge, nor will judge. The pupil is one whom the teacher likes to trust; all are welcome to the teacher. The teacher is spiritually mother and father to the pupil. The life of the teacher is often a sacrifice; they are often persecuted and suffer a great deal. What little help the teacher can give, they will give.

There is no special qualification needed to become a pupil. The teacher gives, but it is for the pupil to receive it. The teaching is like a precious jewel hidden in a stone; it is for the pupil to find the jewel within the stone.

In the East, inner teaching is part of religion. In the West, education is valued. We need a sacred education. In Sufism, a *murshid* will teach or give instructions and the pupil may practice something based on those instructions for a month, or even a year. We cannot have a different practice for every week. My grandfather practiced one particular meditation for forty years, and then a miracle happened to him. We must not be over-eager for new practices before having had a result from the first one, and we must promise not to reveal our practices.

One part of the study of Sufism is for initiates, the other for non-initiates. Only a *murshid* can give initiation; but study can be led by others who know how to conduct it for a time. Notes should not be taken, for that which is heard and seen is twice as profitable. Sometimes the depth of a teaching, unseen at first, is understood later. I sang a *mantra* for fifteen years without understanding it, when suddenly it was revealed within me. There is a teacher in every one of us that teaches when the time comes.

We have a tendency toward argumentation, but it should not become a hobby. No one attains peace by fighting. The lessons are not for debate; the spirit in us must ponder them. If there are mistakes in them, they come from the *murshid*, not from the one who speaks through us. The credit of all good and wisdom belongs to God, not to human beings. Do not dispute; take it or leave it. Make use of that with which you are at one and forget that which does not appeal to you. This Message has been destined for humanity in general and not to a particular people. What I give to you, give to others.

Notes on Gatheka XII

1. *Everyone has a 'devil' in them, and everyone has an 'angel.' Everyone is at once human and animal.*

That is to say, everyone of us has, in Jungian terms, a "shadow" accompanying what is illuminated and cherished in us. Likewise, the human being is a species of animal with distinctly human characteristics, and also basic animal characteristics and drives.

2. *We must discover when we have manifested or are manifesting our 'devil' or animal nature. What we want to manifest is a human spirit.*

Inayat Khan, again mirroring Jungian psychology, is suggesting bringing the 'unconscious' or 'shadow' into awareness, and taking responsibility for it. However, in desiring to emphasize the "human spirit," we are not at the same time disregarding or disparaging our "animal nature." That must be 'owned' and honored, too. Nevertheless, we must not live in the animal to the exclusion of the human. The human characteristics (our most unique characteristics as a particular species of animal) must be central to our lives, or we end up living beneath our possibility and responsibility.

GATHEKA XIII
THE DOCTRINE OF RECIPROCITY

In Hindu and Buddhist thought, the doctrine of *karma*—reciprocity[1]—is emphasized more than in the religions of Bani Isra'il, meaning Judaism, Christianity, and Islam.[2] The whole basis of Hindu philosophy is the doctrine of *karma*; but the moral of Bani Isra'il is also based upon reciprocity. On one side, the *moral* is based on reciprocity; on the other side, the *philosophy* is based on reciprocity.

What is the meaning of the word *karma?* The meaning is 'action.' It is evident that what you sow, you also reap (Gal. 6:7); the present is an echo of the past, the future is a reflection of the present. Therefore, it is logical that the past makes the present and the present makes the future.

Nevertheless, among Sufis, little has been said on this subject. Why does Sufism not speak on the subject? Is it opposed to it?

The answer is that Sufism is not at all opposed to the doctrine of reciprocity; but in the way a Sufi looks at it, one cannot help but close one's lips.

In the first place, what we call 'right' or 'wrong' is conceived according to our own knowledge. We call something 'right' which we think is right, and which we have learned to call 'right.' We call something 'wrong' which we have learned to call 'wrong.' In this way, various communities, nations, and peoples differ in their conceptions of right and wrong. We accuse another of doing 'wrong' on the grounds that *we* know it is wrong. How do we know it is wrong? Because we have read it in a book, or been told that it is wrong, or learned that it is wrong. We look with horror and prejudice at the customs of other individuals, communities, and nations; but what is the actual label, stamp, or seal upon them that makes them 'right' or 'wrong'?

At every stage of evolution, our conception of good and bad, right and wrong, changes. How does it change? Do we see *more* or *less* wrong as we evolve? One might think that by virtue of one's evolution one might see more wrong, but that is not the case. The more we evolve, the less wrong we see. It is not always the action that matters, but the motive behind it. An action which appears 'right' may be made wrong by the motive behind it. An action which appears 'wrong' may be right by the motive behind it. The ignorant are ready to form definite opinions about another's actions, but the wise find it difficult to form such an opinion.

How does this relate to religion? As a person evolves spiritually, as we have said, they see less and less wrong, so how can we think of God as going about counting all the little faults of human beings? We read in the New Testament, "God is love." (1 John 4:8) What is that love? Love is forgiveness; love is not judgmental. When people make God into a cruel judge, sitting in the seat of judgment reviewing every human fault, judging every action and handing out sentences of punishment, casting people from heaven, what happens to the God of love?

Leaving religion aside for a moment and considering things from a philosophical perspective, we might ask the question: are we machines or engineers? If we are machines, we are not responsible for our actions and are acted upon mechanically. If we are engineers, then we are responsible. If we are responsible for our actions, then we are masters of our actions and our destiny. If we are engineers, then we make our destinies as we wish.

Taking this point of view, the Sufi says, 'If things are wrong with me, it is the effect of my actions. But that does not mean that I should submit or resign myself to destiny. I must make my destiny, because I am the engineer.'

I once heard someone say: "I have been ill for years, but I am resigned to it. I took it easily because it is my *karma* I am paying back." But, by this reasoning, they may have actually prolonged the "paying"! What was perhaps to last ten years may have lasted a lifetime. The Sufi, on the other hand, is both the patient and the doctor, asking the questions: 'Is my condition bad? Is it the effect of the past? I will try to cure it. The past created the present; but with this present, I will make the future.' Sufis do not allow the influence of the past to overpower their lives; Sufis want to produce the influences in the present to make their lives better.

Before you take upon yourself the responsibility for paying back the past, you must ask yourself, 'What was I in the past?' How can you be responsible for what you do not know? Conscience informs responsibility. That is a sufficient load to carry in life.

When you look at yourself philosophically, what do you find? The keener your sight becomes, the less you find of yourself. The more conscious of reality you become, the less conscious you are of yourself. The burden of the past is taken up without an invitation. It gives you no benefit; it is only the satisfaction of justifying circumstances. The pain that might have been finished continues because you fortify it.

The principle object of esoteric work is to transcend the more limited notions of yourself. Think about life as a whole— what it is, what it has been, and what it will be. This produces a synthetic point of view. It unites instead of separating. It is constructive. The secret of spiritual liberation is to be found in this.

The Brahmins, Vedantists, and Buddhists, who expound the doctrine of *karma*, in attaining the goal they call *mukti*³ or *nirvana*, also rise above the notion of *karma*. Unless a person rises above that idea, they do not reach *nirvana*. *Nirvana* means 'no' *(nir)* 'color' *(vana)*—'no color,' no label, no division.⁴ Seeing all of life as one is the secret of *nirvana*.

Notes on Gatheka XIII

1. *In Hindu and Buddhist thought, the doctrine of* karma—*reciprocity* . . .

Karma is a Sanskrit word that simply means 'action.' However, it has the connotation of meaning, an action and its reciprocal consequences.

2. . . . *the religions of Bani Isra'il, meaning Judaism, Christianity, and Islam.*

Bani is Arabic for family or 'the children of.' In traditional Islamic studies, *Isra'iliyyat* is the word used for material related to Judaism or from Jewish sources, and often applies to Christian and Zoroastrian materials as well. Inayat Khan's use of "Bani Isra'il" seems to be an extension of this usage.

3. *The Brahmins, Vedantists, and Buddhists, who expound the doctrine of* karma, *in attaining the goal they call* mukti . . .

Mukti is Sanskrit for 'liberation' or 'release,' and refers to one who is spiritually liberated from the bondage of misconceiving reality.

4. Nirvana *means 'no'* (nir) *'color'* (vana)—*'no color,' no label, no division.*

Another explanation of the Sanskrit word *nirvana* is 'extinguished,' 'blown out' (from the verb root, *va*-, 'to blow,' and *nir*, 'out'), as if no longer consuming the fuel of afflictive emotions and being consumed by the fires they cause.

GATHEKA XIV
THE LAW OF LIFE
Inner Journey & Outer Action

A person *arrives* at all that comes to them. I do not mean to say that they do not make it, create it, earn it, deserve it, or that it does not come by chance; all that comes to one may come in these ways; but, at the same time, a person 'arrives' at it.

Making, creating, earning, deserving, and chance are the means through which a certain effect is achieved; but what brings that effect about in reality is the person. This subtle idea remains hidden until we gain insight into the law of life and see its inner workings. For instance, we could say that someone came into a certain position or rank, or into possession of wealth or fame, by working for it. Outwardly, that might be true; and yet, many people work hard and do not arrive at such positions or ranks, wealth, or fame. We could also say that all providential blessings come to those who deserve them. But we see so much in life that actually contradicts this idea. There are many in the world who are undeserving, and yet, obtain their desires.

Every appearance of free will in life also seems to be accompanied by helplessness, and a deeper insight into life will also prove that what seems to be chance is not so in reality. It seems to be chance only because illusion is part and parcel of the nature of life.

GATHEKAS

What do I mean by 'arriving' at a certain thing? Every soul is continually making its way toward something, sometimes consciously, sometimes unconsciously. What a person does outwardly is an appearance of action, an action that may have no connection with one's inner working. This is like a journey: not everyone knows what they are making their way toward, and yet everyone is making their way. Whether they are making their way toward the goal they desire, or making their way toward quite the opposite goal, which they never desired, they do not know.

When a goal is realized on the physical plane, a person is sometimes conscious—'I have not worked for it. I have not created it. I have not deserved it. I have not earned it. How is it possible that this has come to me?' If it is something desired, perhaps they will credit it to themselves and try to believe, 'I made it happen in some way.' If it is undesirable, they may attribute it to someone else, or suspect that it happened for some other reason. In reality, it is a destination at which they have arrived at the end of a journey: they cannot say with any certainty that they created it, made it, deserved it, or that it has come by accident. What can be said is that they have journeyed toward it, either consciously or unconsciously, and have arrived at it. Therefore, in point of fact, no one—either in desirable or undesirable experiences—has departed from the destination at which they were meant to arrive.

What is most necessary is to connect the outward action with the inward journey. The harmonizing of these will cause ease and comfort. You must have harmony within yourself. Once this harmony is established, you can begin to see the cause of all things more clearly than you can in its absence.

You might ask in what way harmony could be established between the inner journey and your outward action. What generally happens is that a person is so absorbed in the outward action that their inner attitude is obscured. It is thus necessary to remove the screen which hides our inner attitude from us.

GATHEKA XIV

Most are conscious of what they do, but not of their inner attitude. In other words, everyone knows what they are doing, but not necessarily where or toward what they are going.

No doubt, the more you are conscious of your inner attitude, the less pronounced your action. Thought controls action, but it only gives a rhythm and a balance to life. Compared with a person who is capable of running, but who does not know where they are going, another who knows where they are going is better off walking slowly.

There are two parts to one action. There is an action in our inner life, and there is an action in our outer life, the inner and outer being. The outer being participates in physical action; the inner being participates in attitude. Both may appear to be actions of free will, but in a certain way, both prove to be mechanical or automatic. The inner action has a great power and influence upon the outer action. A person may be busy in some action all day, but if their attitude is working against them, they may never succeed in the work.

Through your outward action, you may deserve a great reward; but in your inner action, you may be undeserving. Therefore, if these two actions are contrary to one another, the desired results may be divided. The most desirable result comes through the harmonizing of these two activities.

GATHEKA XV
Sufi Mysticism II
Gaining Understanding with the Mind

The knowledge a mystic attains prepares them to find their way to the truth. Reasoning is a faculty the mystic develops. The mystic does not stop at the first reason discovered, but seeks the reason behind all reasons. Therefore, in everything, whether right or wrong, the mystic inquires into the reason. The immediate answer is unsatisfactory; the mystic sees reasons behind the reasons. The mystic advances in the knowledge of all things, knowledge far greater than the knowledge gained by one reason alone.

Neither right nor wrong, good nor evil, excites the mystic much, nor gives the mystic a great shock or surprise. Everything seems to have a nature; and it is through understanding these natures which makes the mystic feel at one with all existing things. What is more desirable in life than understanding? Understanding brings harmony to your home, with those near and dear to you, and peace outside your home with many others of different natures and character. If you lack understanding, you are poor in spite of all you possess; it is understanding which makes you 'rich.'

If you could picture *life* itself, it would look like a sea in a storm, with waves going back and forth. Understanding this gives you the weight, the ballast to endure these waves, the rain and storm, and all the vicissitudes of life. Without understanding, you are like a boat tossed on the waves of the sea, too light to endure the dramatic storm. Through understanding, a mystic learns. The mystic learns tact and is tactful in all circumstances. The mystic's tact is like a ship with a heavy load, well-ballasted; the wind cannot overturn it; it holds firm in the midst of the storm on the sea.

The nature of life is such that it easily excites the mind and can make a person unhappy in the space of a single moment. It makes people confused, so that they do not know where to step next. The mystic, on the other hand, stands still and looks into the secret of life, seeking it in every experience, in every failure and success; from each the mystic learns a lesson. Therefore, both failure and success are profitable to a mystic.[1]

The mystic knows every heart and every nature; whereas others, untouched by the mystic's secret, suffer much difficulty at home and outside, lacking this understanding. They dread the presence of those they do not understand; they want to run away; and if they cannot escape, they feel as if they are in the mouth of a dragon. If placed in a situation they cannot easily change, they become confused, heaping confusion upon confusion.

Often, where two people do not understand one another, a third person helps them to understand each other, and the light thrown upon them brings about greater harmony. The mystic says, 'Whether it is agreeable or disagreeable, make the best of it; try to understand how to deal appropriately with such a situation.' A life without understanding is like sitting in a dark room that contains everything you desire; it is all there, but there is no light to see it.

Though there are many souls who might wish to leave this world, the world is a place of wonder. There is nothing which may not be obtained in it. It is all here . . . all things good and beautiful, all things precious and worthwhile, if you know their nature, their character, and how to obtain them.[2]

Gatheka XV

The work of the mystic, therefore, is to study life. For the mystic, life is not a play, or for entertainment. For the mystic, it is a school for learning in every moment. It is a continual study. Therefore, the scripture of the mystic is human nature itself. Every morning the mystic turns a new page in this scripture.

The prophets have brought the Message to the world at different times, and their books have become scriptures, lasting thousands of years.[3] Generations have taken their spiritual sustenance from them.

The mystic respects all religions, understanding all their different and contrary ideas, for they understand everyone's language. The mystic can agree, without dispute, with the wise, the foolish, and the simple; for the mystic sees from every point of view. This is why they are harmonious with all. A person comes to a mystic and says, 'I cannot believe in a personal God; God means nothing to me.' The mystic answers, 'I understand.' Another says, 'God is only intelligible in the form of the human being.' The mystic says, 'That's true.' And another says, 'God is above comprehension; this idea of a personal God is foolish!' And the mystic says, 'You're right.' For a mystic understands the reason behind all the opposing arguments.

A missionary once approached a Sufi in Persia, wanting to confirm his own understanding of Sufi teachings. The Sufi sat quietly with two or three disciples while the missionary asked a few questions and gave his own point of view. The Sufi then answered, "You are right." But the man wanted to argue with him and pressed him for some dissent. Still, the Sufi only said, "That is true, too." The missionary tried again, hoping to finally engage the Sufi in an argument, but he was disappointed. There was no opportunity for argument, as the Sufi saw the truth in everything he said.

The truth is like a piano. The notes may be high or low, you may strike a C or an E, but they are all notes. The difference between ideas is also like that between musical notes. In daily life, if we have the wrong attitude, all things are wrong; if we have the right attitude, all things are right. Those who do not trust themselves will not trust even their best friend. Those who do trust themselves, will trust everyone.

Things which seem to be completely separate, like right and wrong, light and darkness, form and shadow, are divided by only a hair's breadth to the mystic. Before the mystic, an outlook opens on life, an outlook which reveals the purpose of life. The question the mystic asks is this—'What is my being? Is it my body? No. The body is my possession. I cannot be that which I possess.' The mystic asks—'Is it my mind? No. The mind is something I possess, too; it is something I witness. There must be a difference between the knower and the known.' In this way, in the end, the Sufi comes to an understanding of the illusory character of all the things one possesses.

Then the mystic begins to think—'It is not my self which thinks, it is the mind. It is the body which suffers, it is not my self.' It is liberating for us to know we are not the mind. One moment I have a good thought, in another moment a bad thought . . . a right thought, a wrong thought, an earthly thought, a thought of heaven. It is like a moving picture, and I who witness it.

Seeing this, the mystic liberates the Self, which, owing to illusion, was buried under the mind and body. What one calls a 'soul' was lost there; it was a 'soul' unaware of the truth that body and mind are the vehicles by which to experience life. In this way, the mystic begins the journey toward immortality.

Notes on Gatheka XV

1. *Therefore, both failure and success are profitable to a mystic.*
   Following this line, we have omitted this paragraph:

   The ideal of a mystic is never to think of disagreeable things. If you do not want something to happen, do not think of it.

GATHEKA XV

The mystic erases all disagreeable things from the past from the mind. The mystic collects and keeps happy experiences and makes a paradise of them. Are there not many unhappy people who keep a part of the past before them that causes them pain in their heart? Past is past; it is gone. Eternity before you. If you want to make your life as you wish, do not think of disagreeable thoughts, or of painful experiences and memories that make you unhappy.

The idea that the mystic does not wish to reify possible, undesirable events by actively engaging them is valid, of course, and discussed elsewhere in the *Gathekas*. However, even if we can support the view of leaving past experiences and "disagreeable things" behind from a certain perspective, that perspective is not balanced here in such a way as to make the reader know that bypassing emotions and difficult memories, without sufficient examination, is not considered healthy from a psychological perspective. Therefore, we have moved this passage to the notes.

2. *It is all here . . . all things good and beautiful, all things precious and worthwhile, if you know their nature, their character, and how to obtain them.*

Following this line, we have omitted this paragraph:

If you ask people, 'What is the nature of life?' they will often say, 'The more we strive for happiness, the more we are removed from it.' This is true. But they are taking the wrong path too if they do not know that unhappiness does not exist. Also, happiness is more natural than unhappiness, just as good is more natural than evil, and health more natural than illness. But people are pessimistic. If you tell them good things about someone, they cannot believe it. If you tell them bad things about someone, they are quick to say, 'Yes, that's true.'

This passage, while consistent with other views expressed in the *Gathekas*, requires more explanation, and is not considered entirely helpful to the reader, as such, appearing to belittle the experience of unhappiness. It is to be remembered that the *Gathekas* are transcriptions of oral talks, where not all thoughts are complete or sufficiently explained.

3. *The prophets have brought the Message to the world at different times, and their books have become scriptures, lasting thousands of years.*

Prophets are here understood in the Islamic sense, as *rusul*, 'messengers, who brought the Message of *tawhid*, 'unity,' which they preserved in books.

GATHEKA XVI
Sufi Mysticism III
Preparing the Heart for the Path of Love

What is the heart, and where is it located? We say the heart is in our breast, and that is true. There is a nerve center in the breast that is deeply connected with our feelings.[1] When we feel great joy, we feel something light up in that center, and we, too, seem lit, as if from within. We feel as if we are flying, and there is a great joy in our life. Likewise, if depression or despair comes into our life, this also has an effect upon that center.

But the heart is not this center alone. It is as if a mirror stands before the heart, facing the heart. Every feeling in the physical being is reflected in this mirror. As people are generally ignorant about the soul, they do not know where their heart is, nor even that center where their feelings are reflected.

Interestingly, scientists know that the physical heart is the first organ to form as the child grows in the womb. Likewise, the mystic also conceives of the heart as the beginning of form, the spirit which makes each of us individual. The depth of that spirit is in reality what we call the heart. The real heart is the deepest depth of our being. But we first connect to it through those impressions we receive from the nerve center in the breast; thus we call that the 'heart.'

These days, people attribute less importance to feeling; they are more reliant on the intellect. The reason for this is that when they meet the intellectual, they generally find a person of greater balance than the person of feeling. This is no doubt true, but the lack of balance is because there is greater power in feeling than in the intellect. The earth is fruitful and creative, but not so alive and powerful as water. The intellect is creative, yet not so powerful as the heart and feeling. In reality, in the end, the intellectual will prove unbalanced, too, especially if there is no feeling attached to the intellect.

We all know people of whom we tend to say, 'I like them,' or 'I admire them; it's too bad their heart is closed.' Those who close their hearts cannot love fully, nor allow others to love them fully. The person who is only intellectual, in time, becomes doubtful, skeptical, unbelieving, and destructive, as there is no heart-power to balance them.

The Sufi considers the heart's devotion best for cultivating spiritual realization. Those who close their hearts to others, close their hearts to God. Jesus Christ did not say, "God is intellect." He said, "God is love."[2] If God can be found anywhere, it is not in any house of worship upon the earth, nor in heaven above; it is in the heart. The surest place to find God is in a loving heart.

With the help of reason, you may act according to a certain moral standard, but that does not make you good. That is merely an artificially constructed 'goodness.' Natural goodness and righteousness are found in the spring of the heart, a spring of virtue from which life arises. If a person lacks goodness, it is not for lack of training; it is because they have not yet found it in themselves.

Goodness is natural. If love is the torch on your path, it shows your what fairness, the word of honor, charity of the heart, and righteousness mean. Have you never seen a young man who, even with all his boisterous tendencies, falls in love with a woman and begins to change his life? Love has a gentling effect. Because he must train for her sake, he abandons things he was never before willing to abandon.

In the same way, forgiveness is not so difficult where there is love. A child comes to its mother having made a thousand mistakes and asks forgiveness. The mother does not even hesitate before forgiving her child; the forgiveness is simply waiting to manifest. You cannot help but be kind when love is present. In love, we can find the point of contact with every soul we meet.

Some people think it is unwise to show tenderness to everyone, because some people are not worthy of trust. If there is goodness, that goodness ought to be manifested to everyone; the doors of the heart should not be closed.

As a mystic, Jesus Christ taught—"You have heard it said, 'Love your neighbor and hate your enemy.' But I tell you, love your enemies and pray for those who persecute you." (Matt. 5:43-44) The Sufi treads the same path. In showing charity of heart to one's neighbors, the Sufi considers this love *from* God; showing love to everyone, the Sufi considers this love *to* God.

In this, the methods of the Sufi and the Yogi differ. The traditional Yogi is not unkind; the Yogi says, 'I love all, but I intend to separate myself from you, for the soul is light and does not wish to grope around in the darkness; it is better to love you from a distance.'[3] The Sufi says, 'It is a trial, but the trial must be *tried;* thus, I will take up my duties everyday as they come to me.'

Whether 'worldly things' are considered important or not, Sufis are attentive to their duty to those who love them, who depend on them, who like and follow them. Likewise, Sufis also seek the best way of engaging those who dislike and despise them. They live '*in* the world' and yet are 'not *of* the world.'[4] In this way, Sufis consider loving each person they encounter as the main principle in the fulfillment of the purpose of life.

The life of those who love their enemies, and yet lack patience with them, is like a burning lantern with little oil; it cannot endure; before long, the flame dies out. Patience is the oil in love.

In the path of love, what is the oil? From beginning to end, unselfishness and self-sacrifice. Those who say, 'It is all give and take' do not know love; they know 'business.' That is a transaction. People say, 'I loved once, but was disappointed,' as someone might say, 'I dug in the earth, but was disappointed to find mud there.' There was mud, yes; but with patience, they would have reached the water, too.

Patience endures, and endurance makes greatness. Endurance makes things valuable, and people great. Imitation gold can be beautiful like real gold, imitation diamonds bright like real diamonds; the difference is that one fails the test of endurance, and the other prevails. Of course, people must not be compared to objects; and yet, the divine in them is revealed through their endurance in the path of love.

Now whom should you love? and how should you love? Whatever you love—whether a beloved, a friend, an ideal, duty, art, or other creatures—you have opened that door through which you must pass to reach that love that is God. The original object of love is an excuse leading to that ideal of love, which is God alone.

Many have said, 'I can love God, but not human beings.' This is like saying to God, 'I love you, but not your image.' Can you hate human beings, in which God's image is found, and yet claim to love God? If you are intolerant and unwilling to sacrifice, can you really claim to love the sustainer of all being?

The first thing to learn is breadth of the heart. The awakening of the heart is the feeling inside it. If there is a sign of true holiness in someone, it is not in the power of their words, not in their lofty position (whether spiritual or intellectual), and not in their magnetism. The proof of the saintly spirit in them is only expressed in the love of others; it is the continuous spring of love from the divine fountain situated in the heart of each person. When that fountain opens, it purifies the heart; it makes the heart transparent to the outer and inner worlds. The heart becomes the vehicle of the soul to see all within and without. We do not communicate with another person, alone, but also with God.

Notes on Gatheka XVI

1. *There is a nerve center in the breast that is deeply connected with our feelings.*

This seems to be a reference to the solar or cardiac plexus. In the system of *lata'if,* or 'subtle centers,' the *latifa qalbiyya.*

2. *Jesus Christ did not say, "God is intellect." He said, "God is love."*

This is actually said by John the Evangelist in 1 John 4:8. Jesus said, "My command is this: love one another as I have loved you." John 15:10.

3. *The traditional Yogi is not unkind; the Yogi says, 'I love all, but I intend to separate myself from you, for the soul is light and does not wish to grope around in the darkness; it is better to love you from a distance.'*

This is the traditional Yogi-ascetic of India, not necessarily the Yogi of Vedanta.

4. *They live 'in the world' and yet are 'not of the world.'*

To be "in the world, but not of it" is a traditional saying, based on John 17:14-18. The night before Jesus' crucifixion, he prays:

I have given them your word, and the world has hated them because they are not of the world, just as I am not of the world. I do not ask that you take them out of the world, but that you keep them from evil. They are not of the world, just as I am not of the world. Sanctify them in the truth; your word is truth. As you sent me into the world, so I have sent them into the world.

GATHEKA XVII
SUFI MYSTICISM IV
Repose to Communicate with the Self

When the mouth closes, the heart begins to speak; when the heart is silent, the soul blazes forth, raising its flame and illuminating your whole life. This shows the mystic the great importance of silence, which is gained by repose.

Few people know the meaning of repose. It is only when we are tired that we see the need of it. But repose is a great necessity and has many aspects. There is the repose you experience when you retire from the activity of everyday life and find yourself alone in your room. You breathe a breath of gratitude after all the experiences of the day, saying, 'I am relieved to be alone.' Behind this there is a far deeper feeling: nothing to attract your mind, nothing which demands your action. At such moments, your soul has a glimpse of true relief, the pleasure of which is inexpressible.

A thoughtful person is reposeful by nature, and a reposeful person thoughtful by nature. Repose makes one more thoughtful, and continual action makes one less so. People who work in telephone, telegraph, or post offices, upon whose mind there is a continual demand, develop impertinence, insolence, and a lack of patience over time. They do not become less sensible; it is just that the lack of repose weakens their sense of control and makes them give in to such things.

Repose is necessary for every soul living on Earth, whatever their grade of evolution or spiritual status. This is the one thing that must be developed in human nature. It is not merely for adults, but must also be taught to children. Education today thinks so much about the different intellectual things the child will need in life, and so little about the repose that is the greatest necessity for the child.

Sometimes cats and dogs show themselves to be more intuitive than human beings; but are these animals capable of more than human beings? No. It is only that human beings do not give themselves enough time to become more intuitive; they do not give themselves enough time to repose. It has often amused me to see that in New York—where one is exhausted by the noise of trains, streetcars, elevators, and factories—they read newspapers while sitting on the train or in the subway! They fill that little time with another action! All this action of the body is not enough; there must also be action in the mind!

Why is that? Is it nervousness, a disease so common now that it has almost become normal? If everyone suffers from the same disease, then the disease is called 'normal.' What is called 'self-control' and 'self-discipline' only comes from the practice of repose. It is not only helpful on the spiritual path, but also in one's practical life, cultivating helpfulness and consideration.

The mystics, therefore, use this method of repose to prepare themselves to tread the spiritual path. The spiritual path is not an outward path; it is inward. Therefore, the laws and journey through it are different from the laws and journey of the outer path. To put it simply, living in communication with oneself is the beginning of the spiritual path. The life of God is found in the innermost self. The voice of the inner self is available to everyone. It is always present, but not everyone hears it. Therefore, the Sufi enters the path by opening communication within and addressing the self. When you have addressed the soul, the soul reproduces that address, the way the singer may hear their own voice and song reproduced on a disc.

Gatheka XVII

Having taken a first step within, you listen to the echo— either of peace or happiness, light or form—whatever you wished to produce. It is produced as soon as you begin to communicate with yourself. This is so different from those who say, 'I cannot help being busy, being sad, or being worried; it's just the way of my mind and soul!'

Sufis have taught this for thousands of years. The path of the Sufi is not to commune with God or fairies, but with one's deepest or innermost self, blowing the inner spark into a divine flame. But Sufis do not stop there; they go further. They remain in a state of repose, brought about by a certain way of sitting and breathing, and by a certain attitude of mind.

In this way, you become conscious of a part of your being that is not the physical body, but above it. The more conscious you become of this, the more you begin to realize the truth, a truth of certainty, of life eternal. Then there is no longer imagination, nor belief, but realization of that experience which is independent of physical life. In this state, one is capable of truly experiencing the phenomena of life.

The Sufi, therefore, does not dabble in 'wonder-working' and 'psychic phenomena.' Once the Sufi realizes the life beyond the physical, then all life is a phenomenon. Every moment, every experience brings the Sufi a realization of the life they have found in their meditations.

GATHEKA XVIII
Sufi Mysticism V
Realizing the Truth

Our being is a mechanism comprised of body and mind. When the mechanism is in order, there is a certain happiness and fullness to life; when anything is wrong with the mechanism, the body falls ill and our peace departs. Just as the mechanism of a clock is wound, allowing it to run for twenty-four hours, the mechanism of our being also needs a kind of 'winding.' In meditation, we seat our bodies in a posture of repose, and likewise, put our minds in a condition of repose; this regulates the workings of our mechanism. In meditation, as with a clock that has been wound, the effect of its good functioning is felt throughout the mechanism, because everything is in order.

Mysticism combines scientific explanation with the *realization* of those things that are taught by religion, things which would otherwise have no meaning to an ordinary person. Therefore, the mystic's belief is not a belief in an external deity that one has not seen, nor is the mystic's worship a mere exterior form which ends when one's prayers are finished. The mystic's pursuit is logical and scientific, and makes good use of the external world. If possible, the mystic will always unite the outer form with the inner mystical conception.

Many people read and talk about 'heaven' and God's 'sovereignty,' but do not know where heaven is; they feel there is a God, but have no evidence for it. Because of this, many intellectuals, who are actually seeking the truth, flee from exterior religion, because they cannot find satisfactory explanations in it. Consequently, they become materialists.

For the mystic, the explanation of all of religion is the investigation of the self. The more we explore the self, the more we understand all religions. We see them in the light and all becomes clear. Sufism is the light that is thrown upon your own religion, like a candle brought into a dark room containing all the things you want. The one thing needed was light.

Yet the mystic is not always ready to give an answer to everyone. Can parents always answer all the questions of their younger children? No. There are questions that can be answered, and there are some which should wait until the questioner is ready to understand the answer.

I used to be fond of a poem that I did not understand; no matter how hard I tried, I could not find a satisfactory explanation for it. But ten years later, in the space of a second, a light was suddenly thrown upon it, and to my endless joy, I understood! You see, everything has its time. People become impatient and demand answers; some things can be answered right away, and some cannot. The answer comes in its time— one has to wait.

Has anyone ever been able to describe God adequately, all the scriptures and prophets notwithstanding? God is an ideal too high and great for words. Can anyone explain love? Or say what truth is? People ask me so often about the 'truth' that I want to write the word in chalk on a brick and put it into their hands, saying, 'Hold this!' If truth is to be attained, it is only when truth itself has begun to speak, which comes about in revelation. Truth reveals itself. Therefore, the Persian word for both 'God' and 'Truth' is *khuda*, which means 'self-revealing.' God is Truth. We can explain neither the first nor the second word.[1]

The only help the mystic can offer is in how to arrive at this revelation. No one can teach revelation; one has to arrive at it oneself. The teacher is only there to guide one to this revelation. And there is only one teacher—God. The greatest masters were the greatest students; they knew how to *become* students.

How does one begin to learn? How is this revelation brought into the consciousness of those who would tread the path of truth? Through 'initiation'—*bay'at*—the trust of someone who guides granted to someone who is walking the path. The walker must be willing to risk the difficulties of the path, to be sincere, faithful, and truthful, while resisting skepticism and pessimism, lest their efforts fall short of their aim. They must come whole-heartedly, or come not at all. Half-heartedness is without value on the path.

Beyond the qualities of sincerity, faith, and truth, some intellectual understanding of the metaphysical aspects of life is also necessary, which some have, but not all. Necessary, too, are the qualities of the heart, all of which are rooted in love, which is itself divine. Then comes action attuned to the path of truth, action that creates greater and greater harmony. And finally, repose; for that which is learned in a year of study may also be learned in the silence of a day, if one only knew the actual way of silence!

Notes on Gatheka XVIII

1. *If truth is to be attained, it is only when truth itself has begun to speak, which comes about in revelation. Truth reveals itself. Therefore, the Persian word for both 'God' and 'Truth' is* khuda, *which means 'self-revealing.' God is Truth. We can explain neither the first nor the second word.*

These statements play on the understanding of God as the Truth, *Allah* as *al-Haqq*. Among Sufis, these are equivalent terms. The Farsi word, *khuda*, is generally understood as 'lord,' 'ruler,' or 'god.'

GATHEKA XIX
Sufi Mysticism VI
The Way Reached by Harmonious Action

People often think that study, meditation, and prayer, alone, can bring them to the goal. But there is a great deal to be done through action. Few know what power every action has upon their life, what power a right action can give them, and what effect a wrong action can have. People usually consider what others think of their actions and not what God thinks of them.

If we knew what effect every act produced upon us, we would understand that, though a murderer may escape the police, they have not escaped their action. We cannot escape ourselves; the true judge is sitting in our own hearts. We cannot hide our actions from ourselves. Not knowing the true conditions of others, it is almost impossible to judge the actions of another person. We can best judge ourselves. However wicked they may seem, people are not pleased with their harmful actions. Even if one is pleased for a moment, the pleasure will not last.

What is 'right' and what is 'wrong'? No one can stamp any deed as 'right' or 'wrong.' But there is a natural sense in us which distinguishes between 'right' and 'wrong,' 'just' or 'unjust,' even in children. One sees the line and color in art or decoration; one notices whether the tablecloth is laid evenly on the table or not, when a line that should be straight is not. There is a natural sense of right in the heart of everyone, the natural instrument that masons use for building a house.

Different religions have taught different morals that were correct for the people of that time. The law of the masses must be respected; but the real conception of right and wrong is tied to one's deepest self. The soul is not pleased with that which is not right. The soul's satisfaction is always in something that gives it the most complete happiness. It requires more than thought; it also action. All religions have been based in action as well as truth. Things both material and spiritual have been accomplished by action. For the mystic, then, action is extremely important.

During my travels, coming into contact with different types of people, and staying with them, I have met some who have never read a book of theology in their lives, let alone studied mysticism. Their whole life has been spent in work, business, and industry, and yet I have felt their spiritual maturity, which came naturally from their correct actions in life. They had achieved a state of purity which others might find by study or meditation.

What is the best road to take in life? What road leads to the ideal of life? The best actions consider harmony a first principle. In all circumstances, all situations, all conditions, try to harmonize with others.

It is easy to say, but difficult to live. Why is it so difficult? The answer is not always that 'people are difficult and inflexible,' but that *we* are inflexible!

The palm tree grows straight, its trunk straight and strong; but with all its strength and goodness, it cannot harmonize with other trees. There are also many good people who are not harmonious. There are many true people, but their truth is not always comforting. They offer the truth like a slap. They are like the palm tree, straight and righteous, and at the same time, inharmonious.

A harmonious person is pliable, and can bend to meet another. In order to harmonize, you have to sacrifice, to bend when you do not want to bend. You have to be more pliable than you are by nature, more clever than you actually are! All these efforts will not succeed unless you make an effort, unless you realize that harmony is essential in life.

Why does a mystic attribute such importance to harmony? Because, for a mystic, one's whole life is a symphony of music, each soul contributing to the symphony, playing a particular part in the music.

Success depends upon your ideal of harmony. Few people pay attention to harmony. They do not know that without it, there is no chance of happiness. Only the harmonious can create happiness, and partake of that happiness. Otherwise, it is hard to find happiness in this world. The fighter has no peace; battle will only increase. It is "the peacemaker" who is "blessed."[1] To make peace with others, you will have to fight with yourself.

Whatever your education or position in life, however many possessions you might have, if there is a single thing lacking in your life and heart, nothing can bring you peace. Consider then the value of harmony. It is the most important factor in life, in everything you think, and everything you do.

Notes on Gatheka XIX

1. *It is "the peacemaker" who is "blessed."*

"Blessed are the peacemakers, for they will be called children of God." Matthew 5:9.

GATHEKA XX
SUFI MYSTICISM VII
Sacralizing Human Action

There are certain activities, such as eating, drinking, sitting, and walking, which are shared with other animals. However, if you do these activities as other animals do, then you have not yet awakened to human nature.

What are the characteristics of human nature?

The very same actions—eating, drinking, sitting, walking, and sleeping—have behind them a light to guide them, a light which makes them characteristic of human nature. For instance, if you think you must not push others when walking, or at least say 'I am sorry' if you do, this already demonstrates a different tendency from other animals. Many animals bump into one another with little thought, or pass one another with caution, and sometimes menace, showing horns or growling instead of bowing and greeting one another formally. Human beings will be different in this regard.

The special characteristics of a human being are consideration, refinement, patience, and thoughtfulness. Once one has practiced these, it leads to a deeper practice of self-sacrifice, which then leads to sacred action. When you sacrifice your time or advantage for the sake of someone you love or respect, your behavior rises above the ordinary standard of human behavior. This is an action from the divine aspect of human nature, where the human being begins to think as

God thinks, and one's actions are gradually sacralized, until they become the actions of God. This is greater than merely believing in God, for one's actions have become the very actions of God.

The awakened soul sees all the doings of human beings as the doings of children of one divine parent. The awakened soul looks upon them as that parent would look upon all the children of the Earth, without thinking of them as 'German,' 'English,' or 'French.' They are all equally dear to that parent.[1] The awakened soul looks at them all, full of forgiveness; and not only for those who deserve it. The awakened soul understands both the deserving and the undeserving, because they understand the reason behind all things.

Seeing good in everyone, and everything, you make an opening for the divine light, which expands, throwing light on all life, making that life a scene of divine sublimity. The mystic develops a broader perspective that changes their actions. They develop a sacred point of view. One cannot help calling it a 'divine' or 'sacred' point of view, as one feels that it is from God. When one does right or wrong, one does the right or wrong to God. This is true religion. There can be no better religion than the religion of God on Earth.

It is this point of view that sacralizes us. When treated badly, we can accept it. If we find a shortcoming in our own actions, we take ourselves to task, for those actions are to God.

The mystic's conception of divinity is not only of a sovereign, a judge, or a creator. The mystical conception of God is as the beloved, the only beloved. To the mystic, all the love, all the sincere devotion given in this world is given to God. This devotion wakens the mystic to the beloved, the only beloved, to whom all love is due.[2]

Notes on Gatheka XX

1. *The awakened soul looks upon them as that parent would look upon all the children of the Earth, without thinking of them as 'German,' 'English,' or 'French.' They are all equally dear to that parent.*

Germany, France, and England, were the primary combatants in World War I, in a period characterized by nationalism and deep distrust based on national identity. Inayat Khan makes many such references to World War I.

2. *To the mystic, all the love, all the sincere devotion given in this world is given to God. This devotion wakens the mystic to the beloved, the only beloved, to whom all love is due.*

I have altered the content deliberately here, both to make the point more simply, but also to change the original tone, which could be interpreted as belittling or patronizing of human relationships. Among Sufis, the point of ultimacy is constant: *the beloved is always God.* However, there are differing perspectives on the relative and absolute, some speaking of 'apparent' and 'real' love, and others believing all love to be real. As both perspectives can be found in the teachings of Inayat Khan, I have brought this passage closer to the middle.

The original says: "To the mystic all the love of this world is like little children playing with their dolls and loving them. Thus they learn the lesson they have to realize later in life of taking care of the home. The mystic learns the same lesson by proving sincere and devoted to all sorts of creatures."

GATHEKA XXI
The Ideals and Aims of Sufism

The word 'Sufi' is significant, being related to the Greek *sophos* or *sophia*, meaning 'wisdom.'[1] In common parlance, many people confuse intellect with wisdom. Wisdom is not mere intellect, but that knowledge which comes from within *combined with intellect*. Therefore, Sufism has never been, in any period of history, a religion with a certain creed; it has always been the essence of every religion, and of all religion. When it was given to the world of Islam, it was presented by the great Sufis of that time in Islamic terms. Indeed, whenever the Sufi ideal is presented to a culture, it is presented in terms of their own understanding, in order to make it intelligible to them.

Sufism is not a dogma or a doctrine, a form, or a ceremony. This does not mean that a Sufi does not make use of doctrine, dogma, ritual, or ceremony. The Sufis make use of it, but they are not bound by it. It is not dogma, doctrine, ceremony, or ritual that makes a Sufi a Sufi; wisdom alone is the province of the Sufi; all other things they use for their convenience and benefit. And yet, the Sufi is not against any creed, doctrine, dogma, ritual, or ceremony. The Sufi is not even against the atheist, having respect for every individual.

The God of the Sufi is the God of all, the ideal, and one's very being. The Christ of a Sufi is also one's ideal. Therefore, no savior is foreign to a Sufi. The Sufi sees the beauty, greatness, and perfection of the human being in the ideal. Therefore, the Sufi does not mind if that ideal is called 'Buddha' by one person, 'Krishna' by another, or 'Muhammad' by yet another. Such names make little difference to the Sufi. The Sufi's ideal does not belong to history or tradition; the Sufi's ideal belongs to the sacred feeling of one's heart.

Given this, how can we dispute the ideals of the different creeds? To dispute historical and traditional points of view is vain, and usually makes little impression upon the other.

The idea of a 'Lord' or sustainer of all, taking the form of each person's ideal, is rooted in the deepest feelings of the heart's devotion. Such an ideal cannot be disputed, argued about, or compared. Therefore, a Sufi considers that the less spoken on the subject, the better, because the Sufi respects the one ideal which is called by different names by different people.

To a Sufi, our own human nature, the natural world, and all life, is a revelation; it is all sacred scripture.[2] Does that mean that we do not esteem the sacred scriptures of humanity? On the contrary, the Sufi holds them just as sacred as the followers of those scriptures. Only, the Sufi believes that all scriptures are interpretations of that one scripture, which is before us constantly, an open book, if we could only read and understand it.

The Sufi's object of worship is beauty. Not merely beauty in form, color, and line, but in all its aspects, from gross to subtle.[3] The Sufi's moral is harmony, harmonizing with one's soul, harmonizing with others.[4] Instead of labeling one action as 'sin' and another as 'virtue,' instead of arguing about 'right' and 'wrong' actions, the Sufi trains, as a musician trains the ear, to see what is harmonious and what lacks harmony in themselves, and in their dealings with others. Developing this understanding of the law of harmony produces in the Sufi that goodness which one calls 'divine.'

Harmony is the sign of life. What is life? Life, in poetic terms, may be called, 'love.' The loveless heart may have religion and knowledge, and yet be lifeless, dead. As the New

Testament says, "God is love." (1 John 4:8) God is in the heart of each person, and the heart of each person is heaven itself. When that heart is closed by the absence of love, then God is unavailable, too. When this heart is open, God is available, and one is alive from that very moment.

In action, conscience is the Sufi's guide. The Sufi seeks justice, continually. The Sufi's method of seeking justice is different from that of others. Others consider whether *they* are treated 'justly' or 'unjustly.' This is the common approach, and keeps one far from true justice. The Sufi knows there is only one justice: if *you* are acting justly (if one can be just at all), and if *you* can satisfy your deepest self with your actions.[5] With this sense of justice, the Sufi is pleased, and that is the Sufi's path.

What is the ultimate aim of the Sufi? The Sufi's ultimate aim is to probe the depths of life, to part the veil that keeps one ignorant of life's secret. The attainment of this secret is the greatest happiness. Seeking the depths of life is how the Sufi seeks God. Realizing this, the Sufi realizes truth. In this truth, one finds the peace for which every soul yearns.

What is the mission and work of Sufis in the world? Do we intend to do away with wars? Do we intend to disarm the world? Do we intend to make one nation? Do we intend to make humanity followers of one religion? Do we intend to make all people 'spiritual'? Are we trying to make all people 'wise'?

All of this is arrogant presumption. Sufis would be the first to call themselves out for such presumption. The world is as it is. All institutions and movements work in whatever way they think best for humanity. Our work is humble service to God and humanity: to call our friends and ourselves to a right attitude, an attitude that will bring everyone different results. But we are not working for any *particular result*; we are working for the cause that will produce results. If a person's attitude does not change, even if better results are achieved, they will not last.

Therefore, we do not force doctrines, dogmas, or principles upon people. Our work is only to present that attitude which is most natural, that which every soul is seeking in the deepest part of its being. It is not new to human nature.

Sufis are friends, belonging to different religions, different nations, and different races, who have united in wisdom and understanding to serve at this juncture in time. The only source of protection, from which we draw energy and courage, is the one source in whose service we devote our lives.

Notes on Gatheka XXI

1. *The word 'Sufi' is itself significant, being related to the Greek* sophos *or* sophia, *meaning 'wisdom.'*

The word 'Sufi' seems most likely to be derived, etymologically speaking, from the Arabic word, *suf,* 'wool,' but Inayat Khan is fond of pointing out its *essential* relationship to the Greek word, *sophos.*

2. *To a Sufi, our nature, the natural world, and all life, is a revelation; it is all sacred scripture.*

The third of Hazrat Inayat Khan's "Ten Thoughts," or the Inayati-Maimuni "Ten Remembrances," says: "There is one holy writing, the sacred book of nature, the only scripture that truly enlightens its reader."

3. *The Sufi's object of worship is beauty. Not merely beauty in form, color, and line, but in all its aspects, from gross to subtle.*

The eighth of Hazrat Inayat Khan's "Ten Thoughts," or the Inayati-Maimuni "Ten Remembrances," says: "There is one object of praise, beauty that lifts the heart of its worshipper through all of its aspects, seen and unseen."

4. *The Sufi's moral is harmony, harmonizing with one's soul, harmonizing with others.*

The seventh of Hazrat Inayat Khan's "Ten Thoughts," or the Inayati-Maimuni "Ten Remembrances," says: "There is one moral, love springing from the transparency of the self and blooming in deeds of loving-kindness."

5. *The Sufi knows there is only one justice: if* you *are acting justly (if one can be just at all), and if* you *can satisfy your deepest self with your actions.*

The fifth of Hazrat Inayat Khan's "Ten Thoughts," or the Inayati-Maimuni "Ten Remembrances," says: "There is one law, the law of reciprocity, observed by a selfless conscience wedded to a sense of awakened justice."

GATHEKA XXII
SERVING THE SUFI MESSAGE

The meaning of the word 'Sufism' is 'wisdom.'[1] Wisdom is a knowledge acquired from within and without. Sufism is not only intuitive knowledge; it is knowledge acquired from life in the world, too. Sufism is not a religion, nor a cult or a doctrine. The best explanation of Sufism is that any person who has a knowledge of life outside and inside is a Sufi. For this reason, there has never been in any period of the world's history a founder of Sufism; and yet, Sufism has always existed.

There have been esoteric schools since the time of Abraham, many of which could be called 'Sufi schools.'[2] The Sufi schools of Arabia developed metaphysics; the Sufi schools of Persia developed poetry and literature; the Sufi schools of India developed the faculty for meditation.[3] But the central theme of Sufism, the truth and ideal, have remained the same in all these schools. The different schools have been called by different names, but all are considered 'Sufi.' These schools exist even now, and it would not be an exaggeration to say that there are millions of souls, followers of different religions, who benefit from the wisdom of these 'schools.'

Every school has its own method, and every method is colored by the personality of the leader. There are schools of dervishes, schools of faqirs, schools of saliks, who teach moral culture with philosophical truth.[4] But here the account of the ancient history of Sufism finishes.

GATHEKAS

Our movement is a movement of the members of different nations and different races united in the ideal of wisdom.[5] Wisdom does not belong to any particular religion or any particular race; wisdom belongs to humanity. It is a sacred property, inherited by everyone. In this realization, we—in spite of different nationalities, races, beliefs, and faiths—still unite and work for humanity in the ideal of wisdom.

There are three aspects of our activity. One aspect is the Sufi Order to which one is admitted by initiation. To what school do we belong? To the world community of the Sufi Order. What method is it? The Sufis of ancient times brought wisdom to the Islamic world and presented that wisdom in Islamic terms. Our school has a broader field of work, and is presented to the followers of all religions, as well as those who have no religion, to both spiritualist and materialist. Therefore, the realm in which the esoteric school of the Sufi Order presents its method is necessarily different and distinct.

Initiates and representatives of this school have a more general idea of Sufism than those belonging to particular schools. However, the central theme is the same. This is not said in order for us to be proud of our broadness; it is said so that we may try to maintain this ideal and not fall short of it. Life on Earth tends to drag us into narrowness; we must fight for continual progress on the spiritual path.

The second aspect of our work is Universal Worship. Religion is a delicate subject; the less spoken about it, the better. And yet, just as no one can live by eating food alone, or without drinking water, no one can live by an esoteric ideal without religion. When someone says, 'I will live the esoteric ideal without the outer religion,' it as if they have said, 'I will live in my soul and not my body.'

Besides providing that religion which is destined to be the religion of today, the great work of this activity is to bring about the possibility of people of different religions worshiping together, for all worship one reality.[6] However great the possibility of opposition may be (every good work must meet with opposition), everyone with a just and clear conscience will certainly approve of the idea behind it.

The third aspect is Kinship. No one with any thought can deny the need for this; and those who deny it do not know what they are denying. The more one studies life in-depth, the more one realizes that all wisdom is summed up in the idea of kinship.[7]

All three works serve the Message. It is not a contrived service; it is destined. As murids advance on the path, so will their witness of the divine hand behind everything.

Having received the 'call' to this path, I answered without anything before me or by my side to encourage me. No words can explain how, in this world of changes and difficulties, I made my way. But, at the same time, I had within me that continual 'voice.'

If there are ninety-nine things to discourage you, there is still one to encourage you. If you believe in the teaching, the guidance, and the advice of your *murshid*, you will believe that it will not even be ten years before you will see these possibilities becoming realities.

The Message is God's answer to humanity. If there were five, five thousand, or five million souls standing beside me, or even if I were standing alone, I would think and speak the same hope. I value the devotion and trust of my murids at this time, when we are so few, because that devotion and trust is more valuable when we are poor and without the goods of this world, yet striving to serve humanity together, hand in hand.

Our sincere answer to the divine call now will prove more successful than if we had all the means that the world can offer. I want my murids to realize their responsibility, and not allow themselves to be discouraged by anything, to feel stronger for the very reason that we are small in number. Remember that unity is strength, and in working for the unity of the world is still greater strength.

Notes on Gatheka XXII

1. *The meaning of the word 'Sufism' is 'wisdom.'*

Once again, though the word 'Sufi' seems most likely to be derived, etymologically speaking, from the Arabic word, *suf*, 'wool,' Inayat Khan wishes to emphasize the essential relationship to the Greek, *sophos*.

2. *There have been esoteric schools since the time of Abraham, many of which could be called 'Sufi schools.'*

A well-known suggestion. Even the classic kabbalistic text, *Sefer Yetzirah*, is attributed to Abraham. Abraham's famous encounter with Malkhitzedek (Melchizedek) might be seen as an esoteric initiation. (Gen. 14:18-20)

3. *The Sufi schools of Arabia developed metaphysics; the Sufi schools of Persia developed poetry and literature; the Sufi schools of India developed the faculty for meditation.*

The work of Ibn 'Arabi might be considered an example of Arabic metaphysics; the writings of Hafez and Ahmad Ghazzali examples of Persian Sufi literature; and the work of Shah Kalim Allah Jahanabadi and Nizam ad-Din Awrangabadi in the Indian Chishti-Nizami-Kalimi lineage as examples of an emphasis on meditation.

4. *There are schools of dervishes, schools of faqirs, schools of saliks, who teach moral culture with philosophical truth.*

Darvish, *faqir*, and *salik* are mostly synonymous terms, roughly equivalent to 'Sufi.'

5. *Our movement is a movement of the members of different nations and different races united in the ideal of wisdom.*

The universalist Sufism of Hazrat Pir-o-Murshid Inayat Khan was often described as the "Sufi Movement" in his time.

110

6. Besides providing that religion that is destined to be the religion of today, the great work of this activity is to bring about the possibility of people of different religions worshiping together, for all worship one reality.

Despite the ambiguity of the first part of this statement, and the many interpretative manifestations of it, what is most clear is that Inayat Khan intended to create a "universal" means by which all peoples could worship together, even while belonging to different religions.

7. The third aspect is Kinship. No one with any thought can deny the need for this; and those who deny it do not know what they are denying. The more one studies life in-depth, the more one realizes that all wisdom is summed up in the idea of kinship.

That is to say, the 'relatedness' of all being, and how we relate to one another, is the ultimate focus of the Message.

GATHEKA XXIII
The Need of Humanity

The Message of this movement of Sufism is a call to humanity to unite in a world kinship beyond the boundaries of caste, creed, race, nation, or religion. This movement has no particular creed, dogma, or doctrine. Its philosophy teaches tolerance and understanding above all things, thus awakening sympathy and the realization that the well-being of one depends on the well-being of all.

The voice of God has always warned and guided humanity through a Message given to the prophets and reformers of all ages, who came in answer to the need of humanity.[1] Every religion, in whatever period it was given, was an answer to the cry of humanity, and accepted as such. As rain falls from the clouds, drawn by the need of the plants and trees below, so the Message responds to the longing of souls seeking guidance.

The battles fought through the ages were chiefly caused by religious differences.[2] The true religious ideal has as its principal aim the harmonizing of humanity in the unity of God. But it has always happened that the religious authorities have used religion for selfish purposes, and thereby destroyed its purpose, turning religion, which was a living spring of eternal life for souls, into something stagnant, something dead.

An increasing materialism and overpowering commercial influence has veiled the heart of humanity from truth and caused great distress. In spite of the great advances of modern civilization, people are beginning to doubt whether humanity is actually progressing.

Humanity *is* progressing. The proof of this progress is seen in many marvelous scientific inventions. But these inventions have also helped us to carry out the greatest disaster in the history of the world—war that has consumed numberless lives, among them a generation who had inherited the culture of many generations before them.[3]

In spite of apparent prosperity and flourishing conditions, there is a total absence of 'the ideal.' The minds of most people seem to be centered in one thing alone—*the struggle of life*. Millions are busily occupied, physically and mentally, every moment of their lives, day and night, collecting wealth, the very nature of which is to pass from hand to hand. As long as they have it in their possession, there is an intoxication with it, making them still more avaricious.

Today, the person who is capable of guarding their own interests to best advantage is considered the most practical. The same is true of nations: each works for its own interest. In any nation, the person of most importance is *not* the one who feels for the welfare of humanity, but the one who stands exclusively for the interest of their party, community, or nation. Patriotism can only be a virtue when it is used as a stepping stone to a universal kinship and community. It is justifiable only if it is made a means to consolidate forces in order to work for the welfare of all. Sadly, patriotism has become a lock upon the heart, so that no 'alien'—only those of one's own kind—may be admitted into a country.

What is missing in modern education, in art and science, and in social, political, and commercial life, is 'the ideal.' The ideal is the secret of heaven and earth, and the mystery hidden behind both humanity and God. Human beings, with all they possess in the objective world, are poor in the absence of the ideal; the poverty of our ideals creates irritation, conflict, and disagreement, and thus also wars and disasters of all kinds.

The greatest necessity for humanity is the exploration of the human *persona*, to find the latent inspiration and power in it, and upon this foundation to build the structure of a life. Life is not only to be lived, but to ennoble you, to allow you to reach that perfection which is the innate yearning of your soul.

The solution to the problem of our day is to awaken the consciousness of humanity to its inherent divinity.

Underlying all religions is the realization of unity. This movement of Sufism intends to foster this awareness in humanity.

Notes on Gatheka XXIII

1. *The voice of God has always warned and guided humanity through a Message given to the prophets and reformers of all ages, who came in answer to the need of humanity.*

In the Qur'an, the prophet is considered a *nadir*, or 'warner,' bringing a warning to the people about the way they are living, and the need for change in it.

2. *The battles fought through the ages were chiefly caused by religious differences.*

I think this might be more accurately phrased in another way: religious differences have been used to justify conflicts through the centuries, conflicts whose underlying causes were political, psychological, and opportunistic.

3. *But these inventions have also helped to carry out the greatest disaster in the history of the world—war that has consumed numberless lives, among them a generation who had inherited the culture of many generation before them.*

This is a reference to World War I.

GATHEKA XXIV
The Duties of a Murid

What is initiation?

It is a sacred trust given by a *murshid* to a *murid*, and a trust given by a *murid* to a *murshid*.

There should exist no wall or barrier after initiation. If there is a wall, then the initiation is no longer an initiation. When the wall is removed by the *murid* and the *murshid*, the next wall to be removed is between God and the worshipper.

The Sufi path is a mystical path, and there are certain thoughts and considerations that should be observed. First, if a secret is entrusted to you, it must be kept as a sacred trust. Second, all the teachings you receive, whether bitter or sweet, are medicine for a patient. Third, everything, including 'illumination,' has a time; real progress depends on the patience of the pupil, a patience matching their eagerness to progress.

The great Sufi, Abu Hamid Ghazzali, says, "To journey in the spiritual path is like shooting an arrow without knowing where it will go and what it will hit." The path of initiation is a path of tests: a test from the initiator, a test from God, a test from the self, and a test from the world. To go through these tests is the proof of real progress for the *murid;* the one who will not is wasting one's time.

The Sufi path implies a chain of initiators supporting the *pir-o-murshid*, the 'master and guide,' who must be regarded and respected as one who has gone further.[1] This is the law of nature and life. A child who is disrespectful to their parents will find the same thing from their children. A soldier who does not observe discipline under the captain or colonel will have the same experience when they are captain or colonel. Will we ever arrive at the desired station without considering and observing that which should be observed? Those who have gone furthest—in music, poetry, thought, or philosophy—have always humbled themselves to receive from those who have gone further.

There are three stages for the *murid* to walk on the spiritual path. The first stage is *receptivity*—to take all that is given, without objecting, 'I will take this, but not that.' The second stage is *assimilation*. The third stage is *consideration*, placing it in the mind, and allowing the mind to see the reason of things. The *murid* who walks consciously and securely through these three stages—*receptivity, assimilation*, and *consideration*—will be successful in the path.

Though hierarchical on the surface, this Message leads to true democracy; for it promises the accomplishment of that goal which is the yearning of every soul. The Sufi believes there is a divine spark in every soul; that itself is what makes democracy. Taking a step forward—with trust and confidence in God, the *murshid*, and that divine spark in one's own heart— one is assured of success in life.

Notes on Gatheka XXIV

1. *The Sufi path implies a chain of initiators supporting the* pir-o-murshid, *the 'master and guide,' who must be regarded and respected as one who has gone further.*

Among Inayati Sufis, a *pir-o-murshid* is the head of an Inayati lineage, a successor to generations of 'masters in chain' who have come before them.

GATHEKA XXV
THE PATH OF DISCIPLESHIP

Discipleship was the way of those who followed Christ and all the great teachers of humanity, but modernity has forgotten this ideal, and most of the ideals associated with parenthood and the elder. The consequences of these changes are such that the world is now in conflict. The troubles between nations, between classes, and the troubles in social and domestic life, all come from the same cause—a lack of ideals.

In the ancient world, the path of discipleship was prescribed for all aspects of life. You are not your body alone, but also your soul. The soul is not born when a child is born; the soul is born through consideration. Your soul is also expressed in consideration.

Some become considerate as children, while others never awaken to consideration. People say, 'Love is divine.' Yes, love is divine; but the expression of love's divinity is in consideration. Love without consideration is not fully divine and quickly loses its fragrance.

Intelligence is not consideration. It is the balancing of love and intelligence that brings about consideration, the action and reaction of love and intelligence. Children who are considerate are more precious than jewels to their parents. The person who is considerate, the friend who is considerate, and all those who are considerate, are profoundly valuable to us.

The path of discipleship is the lesson in consideration taught by spiritual teachers. The greatest teachers have not wanted disciples for themselves, or devotion. If any teacher expected such discipleship or devotion, they could not be a true spiritual teacher. How can a *spiritual* teacher be *dependent* on respect, devotion, or consideration from a pupil? The teacher must be above that. Consideration is taught for the *disciple's* benefit, as an attribute that must be cultivated.

In India, consideration and respect was the custom. When I was first sent to school as a child, the first thing my parents taught me was respect, consideration, and a kindly attitude to my teacher.

The prophet Muhammad taught his disciples that the greatest debt everyone has to pay is to their mother.[1] If you want forgiveness, you must act in such a way that before your mother passes from the Earth, she will say to you, 'I have forgiven the debt.' It is not for you to say, 'I have paid it,' whether by money or service. No. Your mother must say, 'I have forgiven the debt.'

What does this teach us? The value of unselfish love which is above all earthly passion.

We inquire within, asking, for what purpose we have come to Earth as human beings? The wise answer from the heart— *We are here to experience life, and to become fully human.* The 'fullness' of humanity is achieved in consideration. Every considerate act is valuable, every considerate word precious. The teaching of Christ—"Blessed are the meek" and the "poor in spirit"— culminates in one thing, *consideration.*[2] Although it seems simple, it is a hard lesson to learn. The more we desire to act according to this ideal, the more we realize that we fail. The further we travel on the path of consideration, the more delicate the eyes of our perception become; we feel sorry for the slightest mistake.

Not every soul takes the trouble to walk this path. Not everyone is a 'plant' willing to grow; many are 'stones.' They do not want to be considerate; they think it too much trouble. Of course the stone has no pain; only the one who *feels* has pain. In feeling, there is life. Life's joy is great, even with pain.

At least the person in pain is alive—unlike the stone! There is a joy in living and feeling which is not expressible in words. After thousands upon thousands of years the life buried in stone and rock has risen to the level of the human being! If you want to be a stone, you had better stay one; but the natural inclination of the living is to develop fully human qualities.

The first lesson a student learns on the path of discipleship is *yaqin*. *Yaqin* means 'confidence.'[3] The student gives or expresses confidence in the human being they consider their teacher and spiritual guide.

There are three classes of confidence:

One student offers or expresses a partial or incomplete confidence, as if wobbling, thinking, 'Yes, I have confidence . . . *Maybe* . . . Maybe not.' This sort of 'confidence' puts you in a difficult position. It would be better not to express such 'confidence,' as it is lukewarm—neither hot nor cold. Moreover, you will do the same in all things—in life and work—alternating trust and doubt, trust and fear, back and forth, neither walking in the air nor on the earth.

There is a second student who gives their confidence to the *teacher*, but who is not sure of *themselves*. They say, 'Yes, I have given my confidence,' but they are not confident inwardly. They have no confidence in themselves; therefore, their confidence is undermined.

A third student gives confidence because they actually feel confident. Only this confidence can rightfully be called *yaqin*.

People of all these categories of 'confidence' were among the disciples of Jesus Christ. Thousands of the first category came and surrounded the master, and later left him. It took no more than a moment for them to be attracted, and less than a moment for them to flee. The second category of disciple persists for some time, just as the drunk persists! Do not think that those of this category did not follow the prophets! Thousands and thousands of such disciples followed the masters and prophets.

Those who stayed to the end of the test were those who, before giving their confidence to the teacher, had confidence in their hearts first! It is they who, if the earth turned to water and the water turned to earth, if the sky came down to earth and the earth rose up to the sky, would stay the same, firm in their truth.

In discipleship one learns a moral: whatever position you assume in life—wife, husband, daughter, son, servant, or friend—a firm and steady confidence is necessary.

After *yaqin* comes a test—*sacrifice*, the ideal in the path of God. No one among the true disciples of the prophet Muhammad thought life too great a sacrifice, if necessary. The story of Ali is well known. Enemies were plotting to kill the prophet Muhammad in his home at night, and Ali had discovered their plot. Urging the prophet Muhammad to escape into the night, Ali himself stayed in the Prophet's home waiting for the assassins, to make it look as if the Prophet were home, in order to throw them off the Prophet's trail. He even slept in the Prophet's own bed, so that the assassins might find *him* there instead! In the end, the enemies touched neither the Prophet nor Ali.[4]

True friendship between teacher and disciple is formed in God and truth forever; nothing in the world can break it. If an apparently 'spiritual link' does not hold, it is a worldly link. It will wear out like a material link. It is the spiritual thought that forms the link between two souls; what else could be so strong as to last here and in the hereafter?

The third lesson in the path of discipleship is modeling, to model one's actions on those of the teacher—in every attitude, with friends, with enemies, with the foolish, and with the wise. If students act only as they wish, and the teacher only acts as they wish, then there is no real long-term benefit to anyone, in spite of sacrifice and devotion.

Remember, no teaching or meditation is so great or valuable as modeling on the teacher in the path of truth. In the imitation of the teacher's attitude and behavior, the entire secret of the spiritual life is hidden, not only the imitation of their outward actions, but also and especially their inward tendencies.

The fourth lesson for the disciple involves turning the inward thought of the teacher outward, until the disciple grows to see in the wise, in the foolish, and in all forms, the teacher.

The fifth lesson for the disciple is to give all that one has given to one's teacher—devotion, sacrifice, service, and respect—to everyone, because one sees one's teacher in all.

One person will learn all five lessons in a short time, and another may not learn them in a lifetime.

A person once went to a Sufi master and said, "I would like to be your disciple."

The master answered, "I will be glad to teach you."

The person was surprised at the master's willingness to accept them, and remarked—"I wonder if you know how many faults I actually have?"

The master replied, "Yes, I know about these faults; but I accept you anyway."

"But I am fond of gambling, master!"

"It doesn't matter that much."

"I am inclined to drink, too; and there are many other faults!"

"I don't mind so much. But, as I have accepted all of your faults, you must accept one condition from me, your teacher."

"Yes, willingly! What is it?"

"You may have all your faults . . . *but not in my presence.* You have to have at least that much respect for your teacher."

The master knew that all five aspects of discipleship were actually natural to the person, and so initiated them then and there.

Soon after, the new disciple went out again to gamble and drink, but unexpectedly saw the face of the master before them wherever they went!

Later, the disciple came to the master, and the master asked them with a smile, "Have you perchance committed any fault since I saw you last?"

The new initiate answered, "No, the problem is that whenever I want to commit any of my usual faults, my *murshid* pursues me!"

Do not think that this spirit must be cultivated, either; it can be found in an innocent child. The other day I asked a child of four, "Have you been naughty," and was amused when they responded, "I would like to be naughty, but my goodness will not let me." This shows us that the spirit of discipleship is actually in us already.

Remember that the teacher is also a disciple. In reality, there is no such thing as a 'spiritual teacher'—God alone is the teacher, and we are all disciples. The lesson we all have to learn is the lesson of discipleship; it is the first and the last lesson.

Notes on Gatheka XXV

1. *The prophet Muhammad taught his disciples that the greatest debt everyone has to pay is to their mother.*

In the Hadith literature, *Sahih al-Bukhari*, 8:2, the prophet Muhammad is reported to have said: "God does not judge you according to your bodies and appearances, but looks into your hearts and observes your deeds." [Someone asked] "Who is more entitled to be treated with the best companionship by me?" The Prophet said, "Your mother." The person asked. "Who is next?" The Prophet said, "Your mother." The person further asked, "Who is next?" The Prophet said, "Your mother."

The person asked for the fourth time, "Who is next?" The Prophet said, "Your father."

2. *The teaching of Christ—"Blessed are the meek" and "the poor in spirit"— culminates in one thing,* consideration.

These are two of the Beatitudes: Matthew 5:5, "Blessed are the meek, for they will inherit the earth"; and Matthew 5:3, "Blessed are the poor in spirit, for theirs is the kingdom of heaven."

3. *The first lesson a student learns on the path of discipleship is* yaqin. Yaqin *means 'confidence.'*

Yaqin is generally translated as 'certainty,' which has the quality of confidence acquired through knowledge, vision, and experience.

4. *Enemies were plotting to kill the prophet Muhammad in his home at night, and Ali had discovered their plot. Urging the prophet Muhammad to escape into the night, Ali himself stayed in the Prophet's home waiting for the assassins, to make it look as if the Prophet were home, in order to throw them off the Prophet's trail. He even slept in the Prophet's own bed, so that the assassins might find* him *there, instead! In the end, the enemies touched neither the Prophet nor Ali.*

See Martin Lings, *Muhammad: His Life Based on the Earliest Sources,* Chapter XXXVI "A Conspiracy."

GATHEKA XXVI
DIVINE MANNER

Among Sufis, the 'divine manner' is called *akhlaq Allah*. We think, speak, and act according to the pitch to which our soul is tuned. The highest note to which our soul can be tuned is the divine note; once we have arrived at that pitch, we begin to express the manner of God in everything we do.

What is the manner of God? It is a sovereign manner, but a sovereignty unknown even to kings and queens. Only the sovereign of heaven and earth knows that manner; but the soul which is tuned to God may express it. It is a manner void of narrowness, free from pride and conceit, and not only beautiful, but beauty itself, for "God is beautiful and loves beauty."[1]

The soul tuned to God becomes beautiful and begins to express God in every action, expressing the divine manner in life.

Why is that considered a 'sovereign' manner?

The word 'sovereign' is often used to signify someone who possesses power and wealth in abundance. But those things which the world seems to value so much begin to lose their allure for the soul tuned to God, who begins to express the divine manner in the form of contentment. To an ordinary person, it might seem as if nothing matters to such a soul—no gain exciting, no loss alarming. Praise is of no consequence, blame of little concern. Honor and insult are all a game. At the end of the game, the gain is not a gain, nor the loss a loss.

What is the value of such contentment?

Such a person is healing, uplifting souls suffering from narrowness and limitation.

Because the nature of life is intoxicating, people often become drunk on it, acting foolish and tyrannical in their desire for that 'drink,' thinking little about others.

In this life, there are so many 'intoxicants'—wealth, passion, anger, possessions. We are not satisfied with possessing material property either, but also try to possess those whom we *pretend* to love. In this way, we become tyrannical and foolish. In reality, we possess none of the things of this world; we are possessed by them, whether wealth, property, a friend, or a position.

The soul exhibiting the divine manner is sober compared with the intoxicated of the world. This soberness produces in us that 'purity' which is called Sufism. Through that purity, God is reflected in the mirror-like soul.

Nothing frightens the soul that reflects God; it is above fright. As it is not possessed by anything, it is not frightened; for all fright is connected with possessions.

Does that mean we should abandon society and all property and go to live in caves in the mountains? No. It is possible to have all the wealth in the world and not be possessed by it; this is the real meaning of 'sovereignty'—nothing binds you, nothing frightens you.

Only that which is truly your own belongs to you. When your soul is your own, all is yours and cannot be taken away from you. Only *you* can take it away. You are your own friend and your own foe. There is no longer pain or suffering, complaint or grudge from without. You are at peace, for you are at home within, whether on earth or in heaven.

The difference between God and humanity is that God is omniscient; whereas, we only know about our own affairs. Being omniscient, God loves all, is interested in all; and so it is with the godly soul. The divine personality expressed through such a soul shows itself in its interest in all, whether known or unknown to that soul. That interest is not inspired by a kindly nature or sympathetic spirit. It does not take interest in another person's welfare and well-being out of duty. It takes an interest because it sees itself in the other. Therefore, the life of another is as one's own person to the godly soul. In the pain of another, that soul sorrows; in the happiness of another, that soul rejoices. Thus, the godly soul largely forgets itself while taking an interest in others.

From one point of view, it is natural for the godly soul to take an interest in others. Those who have emptied themselves of what is called 'self' (in the ordinary sense of the word) are alone capable of knowing the true condition of others. Sometimes they know more about the person than the person knows about themselves, as a physician has more knowledge of a patient's illness than the patient.

The divine manner, therefore, is not like that of parents toward children, or of a friend toward a beloved friend, or a sovereign to a servant, or a servant to a master. The divine manner consists of all manners; it is expressive of every form of love. If it has any peculiarity, that peculiarity is a divine one. In every other form of love and affection, the self is somewhere hidden, asking for appreciation, for reciprocity, for recognition.

The divine manner is above all this. It gives all and asks nothing in return—in any manner or form—thus proving the action of God through the human being.

Notes on Gatheka XXVI

1. *It is a manner void of narrowness, free from pride and conceit, and not only beautiful, but beauty itself, for "God is beautiful and loves beauty."*
Sahih Muslim, 131.

2. *This soberness produces in us that 'purity' which is called Sufism.*

See Gatheka I: "The word 'Sufi' is derived from the Arabic word *safa*, which literally means, 'pure.' That is to say, the Sufi is pure from distinctions and differences."

GATHEKA XXVII
OUR SACRED TASK—THE MESSAGE

Our task as travelers of the Sufi path, and as servants of the divine cause, is to awaken a spirit of tolerance for different religions and their scriptures, to awaken the ideal of devotion to one another, fostering understanding between people of different nations, races, communities, and classes. We do not mean to say that all races and nations must become one, or that there should only be one class;[1] but whatever our religion, nation, race, or class, our most sacred duty is to work *for* one another, in one another's interest, and to consider this the service of God.

We must create a spirit of reciprocity among people of different races, nations, classes, and communities. The happiness, prosperity, and welfare of each of us depends upon the happiness, prosperity, and welfare of all of us. The central theme of the divine Message is simple, and yet difficult—to bring about the realization of divinity in the world and the human soul, which has been overlooked up to now because the time was not yet ripe for this realization. The principal objective of the Message in this time is to create the realization of the divine spark in every soul, so that every soul, according to its evolution, may begin to realize for itself the spark of divinity within. This is the task before us.

What is the Message? The whole of humanity is one single body, and all nations, communities, and races are the different organs.[2] The happiness and well-being of each is the happiness and well-being of the whole. If there is one organ of the body in pain, the whole body has to sustain a share of its strain.[3] Our own welfare and well-being is dependent on, and assured by, looking after others. When there is reciprocity, love, and goodness toward one another, a better time will come.

But how are we to set to work? It is a difficult question to answer; we all have our own way of working, and no one way is suitable for all. Whatever the approach, a great sacrifice will be required to accomplish the welfare and well-being of all. It will require resolve in the face of opposition from friends and acquaintances; there will be monetary sacrifices, too, as needs arise. A great deal of time will have to be sacrificed, as well as the desire for appreciation; the only reward for the work will be the satisfaction of accomplishment. You will be hindered by those who oppose you and those who sympathize, by the bitterness of some and the ignorance of others.[4] If you are too sensitive, it will be easy to take up the work one day and give it up the next! It will take courage to go on in the face of opposition.

A great deal of prudence will be necessary. Without it, the work cannot be successful. Indeed, it will suffer. One needs prudence in dealing with strangers and opponents, and even with your dearest friends. More than anything, we need prudence in this work.

We must work quietly and unassumingly; this task cannot be accomplished by the noise of drums. The less we are known, the better; our reward is gained in being unknown. In being known, we make more enemies; it is not our aim in life to be known. Publicity is not our reward; our reward is being allowed to work quietly by providence. If no one in the world knows of our work, we should not mind. It is God's work, and God's name should be glorified. The glory of God is our satisfaction. The work is done for the benefit of humanity and for the well-being of the world.

Gatheka XXVII

What does it matter if we work and others become known, or if we sow and others reap the harvest? It is always our work and mission to sow and leave the harvest to others.

Forbearance will be necessary with those who persecute you and obstruct the work. People will speak against you, and it will take a great deal of strength to tolerate them instead of defending the 'self.' We are not here for fighting, arguing, or defending ourselves. We are here to work. If someone says, 'You are right,' say, 'Thank you.' If someone says, 'You are wrong,' say, 'Yes, thank you.' If someone says, 'You do good,' say, 'Thank you.' If someone says, 'You do wrong,' say, 'Yes, thank you.' That is it—no defense is necessary. What is the use? How long will you defend yourself? Against how many people? Against one? Against twenty? How much time will you spend on it? If you spend all your time defending yourself against one opinion or another, when will you do your work? Thus, it is helpful to work quietly; in some cases, secretly, so that no one knows you are doing it, the only satisfaction being the accomplishment of a sacred task.

I am saying all of this to make things clear and easy. If it were merely a human enterprise, its outcome would be uncertain; but it is not—*it must be accomplished, and it will be accomplished.* Those of us who are privileged to serve the cause need not seek an intentionally difficult path, but may as well find the simplest and easiest way forward. Greatness is in humility, wisdom in modesty, success in sacrifice, truth in silence. Therefore, the best way of doing the work is to do all we can, to do it thoroughly, to do it wholeheartedly, and do it quietly.

Notes on Gatheka XXVII

1. *We do not mean to say that all races and nations must become one, or that there should only be one class . . .*

That is to say, he is not advocating Communism.

133

2. What is the Message? The whole of humanity is one single body, and all nations, communities, and races are the different organs.

The *risala*, or 'Message,' according to Islamic teaching, has always been—from generation-to-generation, culture-to-culture, prophet-to-prophet—*tawhid*, 'unity.' The idea of *tawhid*, taken to its logical non-dual conclusions by Ibn 'Arabi and Sufism, is expressed by the phrase, *wahdat al-wujud*, the 'unity of all being.' Here and elsewhere, Inayat Khan emphasizes the social implications of this teaching.

3. The whole of humanity is one single body, and all nations, communities, and races are the different organs. The happiness and well-being of each is the happiness and well-being of the whole. If there is one organ of the body in pain, the whole body has to sustain a share of its strain.

This parallels exactly the "organismic" metaphor of Pir-o-Murshid Zalman Sulayman Schachter-Shalomi, where "every religion is a vital organ of the planet," the healthy support of each by the others ultimately leading to the health of the whole 'body.'

4. You will be hindered by those who oppose you and those who sympathize, by the bitterness of some and the ignorance of others.

In his prayer, "Du'a," Inayat Khan says, "Save me, my sustainer, from all manner of injury coming from the bitterness of my adversaries, and from the ignorance of my loving friends." It is not only our enemies who obstruct us, but also the good intentions of our friends and acquaintances.

GATHEKA XXVIII
Sufi Initiation

The word 'initiation' is often misunderstood. Many think it is an entry into a secret society, or a test or trial, or a mysterious phenomenon; but none of these are entirely correct. Initiation, in the terminology of Sufism, is called *bay'ah*, an 'oath' or 'pledge.' No doubt, the English word 'initiation' also refers to a mystery, for the meaning of the word suggests taking initiative, advancing, or moving forward.

Progress is life and stillness is death. Whatever our grade of evolution, it is always advisable to move forward and make progress, in business or the professions, in society or political life, in religion or spirituality.

There is a danger, however, of being too enthusiastic in moving forward. Those who are too enthusiastic may, instead of benefiting themselves, harm themselves in their worldly or spiritual work. There is a time for everything, and patience is necessary in every endeavor.[1] A cook who increases the flame in order to cook their food more quickly often burns it. This rule applies in all things. With small children, parents are often anxious and enthusiastic, thinking their children can learn and understand every good and interesting thing in the world. But such enthusiasm can be problematic; we must give time and space to all things. The first and most important lesson in life is patience; we must begin all things with patience.

The Sufi path is primarily esoteric. In the East, there are three well-known esoteric schools: the Mahayana and Vajrayana schools of Buddhism, the Vedanta schools of Hinduism, and the Sufi schools of Islam.[2] Meditation and contemplation are used in all three, the science of breath being the foundation of each.[3] The schools of Buddhism and Hinduism use asceticism as their principal means of spiritual advancement. The peculiarity of the Sufi schools is that they engage with humanity as a path for spiritual advancement.[4] The realization of truth is not different among them, but Sufism presents truth in a different manner. It is the same form in which Jesus Christ gave his teaching, and the form adopted by the prophets of Israel.

Sufis do not believe we are created to live the lives of angels, nor the lives of animals. Angels are created to be angels, and animals to be animals. For Sufis, the first thing necessary in life is to prove to ourselves to what extent we can be human! And yet, this spiritual development is not merely individual, but concerns all of humanity. What is your relationship to your neighbors? Your friends? To those who depend on you? To those who look to you for help? To strangers? How do you relate to those who are younger than you? Older than you? To those who like and praise you? Those who dislike and criticize you? How do you think, feel, and act in life? Are you moving toward that goal which is the goal of every soul in the world?

For Sufis, it is not necessary to seek the wilderness for meditation; Sufis can do their work in the world, too. Sufis need not prove themselves by extraordinary powers, miracles, exceptional spiritual claims or demonstrations. A Sufi's proof is within, a matter of conscience, observing oneself amidst the struggle of life in this world.

Some people are content with the beliefs they were taught at home or in their houses of worship. They can rest in that understanding until an impulse is born in their hearts to go on higher or deeper. Sufis do not force their beliefs or thinking on such souls. In the East, it is sometimes said that it is a great sin to wake someone who is asleep. There are many in this world who seem to be awake externally, but who are inwardly asleep.

For some, sleep is good and healing. Sufism is for those who are stirring from their sleep, or who have had enough sleep and are ready to rise. What Sufism offers is the real initiation.

There are things which go beyond ordinary comprehension, things you cannot teach with words or even actions. *Tawajjeh* is teaching without words.[5] It is not external teaching; it is a teaching in silence. How can we explain the spirit of sincerity or the spirit of gratefulness?

How can we explain the ultimate truth, or God? All attempts fail, making some confused and causing others to abandon their belief. It is not necessarily that the one who explains does not understand, but that words are inadequate to explain God.

In India, many great sages and saints have been known to sit still in silence for years. We call such a sage a *muni*, one who takes a vow of silence. Some may think judgmentally, 'What a life! Silent and doing nothing!' But some can accomplish more with their silence than others can with ten years of talking. One person can talk about a problem for months and not be able to solve or explain it, and another can find illumination in a moment.

Of course, no one can give illumination to another; it is something that every heart has within it. But the teacher can illuminate (with their own light) the light hidden in the heart of a disciple in initiation. If that light is not available, however, it is not the fault of the teacher. There is a Persian verse by Hafez, which says, "However great the teacher, before the one whose heart is closed, the teacher is helpless." Initiation is an initiative on the part of the disciple *and* the teacher, a step forward on the path of both. On the path of the teacher, the step is to trust the disciple and raise them up; on the path of the disciple, the step is to open their heart, removing the barriers there, allowing nothing to hinder the teacher.

In ancient times, the disciples of the great teachers learned by a method different than the academic method of today's students. With an open heart, perfect confidence and trust, they watched every move the teacher made toward friends and people who looked at them with contempt; they watched their teacher in times of trouble and pain to see how they withstood it all.[6] They saw how patient the teacher had been in arguing with those who did not understand, and how wise the teacher had been to answer everyone gently in their own language. They observed the mother-spirit, the father-spirit, the brother-spirit, the sister-spirit, the child-spirit, the friend-spirit, the forgiving kindness, the tolerant nature, the respect for the elderly, the compassion for all, and the thorough understanding of human nature. The disciples learned that all disputes and books on metaphysics can never teach all the thoughts and philosophy that arise in a person's heart. A person may study everything for a thousand years, or go to the source and touch the root of all wisdom and all knowledge. In the center of the emblem of this Sufi path there is a heart; for from the heart a spring of divine knowledge and inspiration rises.[7]

Two things are necessary on the path of Sufi initiation: contemplation and living the life of a Sufi. Each depends on the other: contemplation helps a Sufi live that life, and that life cultivates contemplation. The question in the West, where life is so busy, and where there is seemingly no end to responsibilities, is whether contemplation is too much to ask when we are tired, even if it is only for ten minutes in the evening. But, for that very reason, contemplation is required in the West even more than the East, where everything, even the surroundings, are helpful for contemplation.

You must start on the path somewhere. If contemplation does not develop in such a way that everything you do in life becomes a contemplation, then contemplation will not do you any good. It is like going to church once a week and forgetting religion the rest of the week. A person who gives ten or twenty minutes to contemplation every evening and forgets it all day will not derive any benefit from it.[8]

Gatheka XXVIII

It is not the Sufi ideal to withdraw into seclusion or sit silent all day; the Sufi ideal is that through contemplation you will be inspired in your study and aspirations, progressing in every aspect of life.[9] This is the proof that your contemplation is the force helping you to withstand all the difficulties that come upon you.

The most important element in the life of a Sufi is friendship, friendship expressed in a tendency toward tolerance and forgiveness of others, service and trust, and a constant desire to love and be a friend to all of humanity.

The Sufi Movement is comprised of an esoteric school, kinship with all of humanity, and worship.[10] In the esoteric school, seekers of truth who wish to follow the path with faith, confidence, and trust are welcome. Peripheral to the esoteric school are kinship and worship. The object of kinship is to unite humanity—currently separated by differences in caste, creed, nation, and race—in the understanding of wisdom. In awakening conscience in ourselves and humanity, we may come to see that the happiness of each person depends on the happiness of all. Our aim, however, is not that all people should become part of the Sufi Movement, but that they may recognize that they are all part of the human family in the parenthood of God.

For those who have some belief but are not satisfied with it, or who desire religion and prayer but do not attend any particular religious service, there is a universal worship. There are some who will not believe unless they are intellectually satisfied; for them, this offers some access to elements of all religions and demonstrates tolerance for different religions and beliefs, so that all may learn to respect the religions of others, religions which have inspired numberless souls, but which are perhaps unknown to them. This unity of religion in prayer and thought is the real kinship of religion—*nature's religion.*

But the central path is the path of initiation. To those entering this central path, kinship and worship are open.

Notes on Gatheka XXVIII

1. *There is a time for everything, and patience is necessary in every endeavor.*

"There is a time for everything, and a season for every activity under the heavens." (Eccle. 3:1)

2. *In the East, there are three well-known esoteric schools: the Mahayana and Vajrayana schools of Buddhism, the Vedanta schools of Hinduism, and the Sufi schools of Islam.*

Originally, this sentence read, "There are three esoteric schools most known in the East: the Buddhist school, the Vedanta school, and the Sufi school." However, each of the three, as generally understood, belong to different categories: Buddhism being a religion, Vedanta a 'school' of Hindu philosophy, and Sufism a supra-normative mystical tradition associated with Islam. Therefore, some clarification is necessary.

When Inayat Khan speaks of "Buddhism" as an "esoteric" school, it is possible that he is referring to the fact that, in most schools of Buddhism, meditation is a foundational practice. And yet, this aspect of Buddhism would not generally be considered "esoteric" within Buddhism; nor would it provide the strongest parallel with Sufism as an "esoteric" or mystical school. What constitutes "esoteric" or "mystical" is in question here. From a Buddhist perspective, those schools of Buddhism showing influences from Yogachara and clear tantric influences might best be described as "esoteric," including Chan, Zen, and Tendai Buddhism, and the Vajrayana Buddhism of Tibet. Thus, I have replaced "Buddhism" with "the Mahayana and Vajrayana schools of Buddhism," which include all of these examples.

Vedanta literally means 'end of the Veda,' and refers to the Upanishads, particular writings grouped together at the end of the Vedas, and which, according to some, represent the essence of the Vedas. The special character of these writings, suggesting the identity of *atman* (self) and *Brahman* (ultimate reality), create the character of the Vedanta schools of Hindu philosophy (which base themselves on a unified understanding of the Upanishads, the Brahma-Sutras, and the Bhagavad-Gita). While the teachings of the Vedanta schools might properly be characterized as "esoteric" and "mystical" from within the Hindu tradition, at least in a certain period, they become more so in the modern use of Vedanta by the Vedanta Society founded by Swami Vivekananda (in many ways, a parallel figure to Inayat Khan), which integrates the Hindu *tantra*. Inayat Khan, who personally knew Vedanta Society swamis in the United States, was likely referring to both the Vedanta schools of Hindu philosophy and the *vedanta* of the Vedanta Society when he says "the Vedanta school."

It is interesting to note that different iterations of these "esoteric schools" have also developed 'universalist' forms that parallel the Sufism of Hazrat Pir-o-Murshid Inayat Khan. Zen Buddhism, as brought to the United States by Shaku Soyen, has transcended its specifically Buddhist origins in some respects, as has Vedanta in the Hindu tradition, under Sri Ramakrishna and his foremost disciple, Swami Vivekananda.

3. Meditation and contemplation are used in all three schools, the science of breath being the foundation of each.

From a certain perspective, this is true of each, and may suggest how Inayat Khan defined "esoteric" in the previous sentence.

4. The schools of Buddhism and Hinduism use asceticism as their principal means of spiritual advancement. The peculiarity of the Sufi schools is that they engage with humanity as a path for spiritual advancement.

This is not entirely accurate for these traditions as a whole, which are as diverse as any other spiritual tradition. Sufism contains strong ascetic currents and has emphasized asceticism in different periods and historical situations, just as the Buddhist and Hindu traditions also have engaged "humanity" in different historical periods and situations. Nevertheless, I suspect that Inayat Khan is not focused on actual "asceticism" in this example, but on the fact that most Buddhist and Hindu schools have emphasized monasticism and a disengagement from 'the world,' while Sufism as a whole (though also emphasizing disengagement from 'the world' on occasion), has never emphasized monasticism, owing to its connection with Islam. According to the prophet Muhammad, "There is no monasticism in Islam." Thus, despite some anti-materialist trends of thought at different times, these trends were ultimately moderated by Islamic norms, to the point that Inayat Khan's non-dualism (based on Ibn 'Arabi) could later stress a sacred engagement with humanity as a path and the purpose of spiritual practice.

5. Tawajjeh *is teaching without words.*

In this case, Inayat Khan seems to be using the term *tawajjeh* in the sense of the Sanskrit, *darshan,* 'seeing,' participating in a silent dialogue or exchange with a holy being. The Arabic *tawajjeh* means 'facing' or 'turning the face toward,' as in God has turned the divine face to you, giving attention to you, establishing connection in the grace of that divine attention (a circumstance also known as *'inayah).* It is also silent dwelling in the acknowledgment of such connection.

6. *In ancient times, the disciples of the great teachers learned by a method different than the academic method of today's students. With an open heart, perfect confidence and trust, they watched every move the teacher made toward friends and people who looked at them with contempt; they watched their teacher in times of trouble and pain to see how they withstood it all.*

One of the most famous anecdotes of the Hasidic tradition concerns Reb Leib Sarah's who, when asked what he came to learn from his teacher, the Maggid of Mezritch, responded, "I came to see how he ties his shoe-laces."

7. *In the center of the emblem of this Sufi path there is a heart; for from the heart a spring of divine knowledge and inspiration rises.*

The common symbol of the Inayati Sufi lineages is a heart with wings, sometimes with a crescent and five pointed star within it.

8. *If contemplation does not develop in such a way that everything you do in life becomes a contemplation, then contemplation will not do you any good. It is like going to church once a week and forgetting religion the rest of the week. A person who gives ten or twenty minutes to contemplation every evening and forgets it all day will not derive any benefit from it.*

This is an important statement and reflection on how spiritual practice is often approached 'in the West,' i.e., as one among many activities meant to benefit a person, rather than as an approach to one's entire life. Thus, a person may meditate occasionally, or even on a daily basis, and still behave poorly in the rest of their life. The seed of meditation does not penetrate one's life because the soil of that life has not been cultivated to receive it. It is the principle difference between what is called a 'mindfulness practice' today and an actual 'spiritual path.'

9. *It is not the Sufi ideal to withdraw into seclusion or sit silent all day; the Sufi ideal is that through contemplation, you will be inspired in your study and aspirations, progressing in every aspect of life.*

The Sufi does practice *khalwah*, or 'seclusion' in silence for specific periods, but for the purpose of cultivating a quality that can be brought back to benefit the world.

10. *The Sufi Movement is comprised of an esoteric school, kinship with all of humanity, and worship.*

During the latter period of Inayat Khan's life, the organization he founded was called "The Sufi Movement." Its core was the "esoteric school," referring to its Sufi teachings and practices. This was another way of saying the *tariqah*, or Sufi 'order.' However, around this hub, he conceived of four spokes, or "activities." "Kinship" was serving humanity as a manifestation of divinity in the social sphere. "Worship" or "Universal Worship" was a universalist religious or interspiritual offering for those who were disaffected with conventional religion but who wished for another option, or for those who were inspired to bring the religions together in a common worship. To these were added "Zirat" and "Healing," emphasizing spiritual ecology and spiritual healing, respectively.

GATHEKA XXIX
WHAT DO WE WANT FROM LIFE?

What do we want from life? Most of us could list a thousand desires. And yet, even after listing those desires, we rarely know what we *really* want. What we *appear* to want is not what we *really* want, because the nature of external life is illusion. As soon as we feel, 'I want this,' the appearance responds, 'Yes, you want me, the appearance!' When we feel something lacking in our lives, we only see the external lack; we do not see the lack within ourselves. What we really lack is an attunement with the infinite and rhythm with the finite, to be in rhythm with the conditions of our lives, and to be in tune with the source of our existence.

Our perpetual complaint in life comes from not being in rhythm with the diverse conditions we face in life. We think that if these situations were to change in accordance with our desires, life would be easier. But that is an immature expectation. If granted our desired conditions, we would also find something lacking in them.

If we look a little more closely at life, we will find that all the 'deficiencies' and 'problems' about which we usually complain add up to something complete and wise, as wise as the 'hands' working behind appearances wish them to be.

There is a Persian proverb that says, "The gardener of the world's garden knows best which plant to rear and which to remove." Some might call this 'fatalism.' But I have no desire to take you any further into fatalism; I want to touch its boundaries, but bring us into the sphere of action. We actually have power to improve our lives, if only we would not lose patience before a desirable condition is brought about, neither abandoning courage nor exhausting hope.

How do we come into rhythm with life and its conditions? Life as it is and our desires are mostly in conflict. If our desires yield to circumstances, then circumstances get the upper hand; if circumstances are mastered, then desire has the upper hand. But circumstances are not always mastered by a conflict or a struggle with them. Caution is needed in 'fighting' the situations of life.

If harmony can be established by peace, it is better to avoid a battle. If you can harmonize with the circumstances of life without struggling, it is better than harmonizing through struggle. Those who complain most about life, and those who are most disappointed and troubled, are those who struggle most with life's circumstances.

Therefore, a weapon is not always required for coming into accord with the circumstances and situations of life; you must try to harmonize with the particular situation first. The great heroes who have fought through life and gained life's 'victory' (in the real sense of the word) have not been those who fought most with its circumstances, but those who made peace with them. The secret of the lives of the great Sufis was that they met circumstances—favorable or unfavorable—with the aim of coming into accord with life's rhythms.

Sometimes desire is a friend, and sometimes an enemy. In unfavorable circumstances, desire is agitated and loses patience; it wants to 'break through' unfavorable circumstances, and often breaks itself. The greatest souls have first offered their hands to their worst enemies; those who make friends of enemies see them as their own selves. A condition as bitter as poison is turned into nectar if we get into rhythm with that condition, understanding it, enduring it with patience, courage, and hope.

When conditions are favorable, we are often afraid that these favorable circumstances will soon pass; but when conditions are unfavorable, we often act as if they will last forever! Why do we do that? *Fear*—fear of those conditions, anxiety about those circumstances, and a desire to get out of them. But in indulging such fears, we lose hope, which is the only thing that keeps us alive in those circumstances.

The nature of life is change, morning till evening, evening till morning. Why then should we not hope that unfavorable circumstances will change and favorable conditions will return? We get into a habit of expecting the worst. Having had bad experiences in life, we expect the worst, saying, 'Nothing good has ever come to me' . . . 'I've always experienced the worst.' . . . 'Everyone has it better than me.' . . . 'I think I was born under an unfavorable star.'

There are many imaginative and intelligent people who, day after day, read the newspaper and draw the conclusion that there is going to be a war. Every little story of struggle gives them the idea that the world is falling apart. Others interested in astrology, going beyond the actual information, expect the end of the world year after year, month after month. It gives them something to talk about at dinner and shocks those who want to live beyond the world's end. Many such predictions and prophecies of danger and the world's destruction have passed, but these prophecies and expectations remain. The best thing you can do is be patient with life's circumstances, understand them with open eyes, and try to rise above them to the best of your ability.

How can we attune to the infinite? The soul can be likened to the string of an instrument. It is attached on one side to the infinite, and on the other to the finite. When we are conscious of the finite, we are tuned with the finite; when we are conscious of the infinite, we are tuned with the infinite. Being in tune with the finite limits us, weakens us, makes us feel hopeless, powerless. But, being in tune with the infinite, we obtain the strength and power to pull through life's adversities.

The work or sacred duty of a Sufi has nothing to do with a particular religion or creed; it is simply to be in rhythm with life's conditions, and in tune with the infinite.

How can you act in accord with life? Instead of fearing life's circumstances, face them and observe them keenly; try to harmonize with them for a time. If circumstances are adverse, try to rise above them.

A young Arab was once sleeping in the field when a serpent happened to slither over his palm. Still asleep, he unknowingly gripped the serpent with all his might. The serpent was thus helpless and could not bite him. When he woke from his sleep, he was suddenly frightened by the sight of the snake in his hand and let it go. As soon as the serpent was out of his hand, it bit him.

Thus, you can manage a situation in your hand better than one you let go. For instance, if you are angry, or have lost your temper in a situation, your natural tendency is to retaliate. The outcome is a struggle, ultimately culminating in loss and disappointment. But when the person with whom you are dealing is angry and has lost their temper, they are actually in a weak and vulnerable position, and that is the time when you can manage them. The situation is 'in your hand.' That person is weak; you are strong.

If you wish to improve your position in life, remember that everything you do affects others. As you elevate yoursel, you run the risk of diminishing the position of others, or of creating unexpected consequences for those near you. For example, a person who wants to be very wealthy, in becoming so (or in maintaining it), often makes slaves of others. This slavery will weigh heavily on them. Our life in this world is dependent on others, and wealth, however powerful it seems to make you, is not really as powerful as it appears. Its power is limited, and it does not really free you from dependencies.

It is not our goal to become resigned to the fact that we will never improve our circumstances in life; but we must first come to terms with our circumstances *as they are* before attempting to improve them. The less conflict there is in the process, the better. For instance, imagine you are traveling through the wilderness and meet a robber who says, 'I'm going to take your life if you don't give me your money.' In order to meet the situation realistically, you must first accept the circumstances; then attempt to get out of the danger with reason and, if possible, without harming the robber. But we cannot always avoid conflict, and we must not turn our backs if conflict is necessary. After all, life is a struggle; and we must be ready to struggle when necessary. Though we must not become so addicted to, or intoxicated with struggle that we lose the way of peace, which is the first, most desirable approach. We must not be like the boxer who is always looking for another person to fight!

What is the other way? Tuning oneself to the infinite in silence and meditation, contemplating what is above and beyond all things of this mortal world, giving a few moments of our lives to that which is the source and goal of us all. In that source alone is the secret of happiness and peace.

Glossary

ādāb (sing. *adab*) – 'etiquette,' 'manners.'

advaita – 'not-two,' 'non-dual.'

advaita vedānta – 'non-dual' school of Hindu philosophy.

ahimsā – 'not-harming.'

akhlaq Allāh – 'manner of God,' 'divine manner.'

ātman – 'self.'

avatār – 'incarnation.'

bāni Isrā'īl – 'family' or 'children of Israel.'

bāwāsāda – 'ever-rising ocean,' 'life of the world.'

bay'ah – 'oath,' 'pledge,' 'agreement,' 'covenant,' or 'deal.' Sufi initiation; also called, 'taking hand.'

bāz – 'falcon.'

bhakti yoga – 'discipline of devotion'

Brahman – 'expanding greater,' 'ultimate reality.'

brahmin – 'of Brahman,' member of the Hindu priestly caste.

darshan – 'seeing,' to have sight of, participating in a silent dialogue or exchange with a holy being.

dervish (darvīsh) – 'one who stands on the threshold.' A beggar. In the Sufi context, a beggar of God, or a mature Sufi.

deus sive natura – 'god or nature,' God as indistinguishable from nature in the thought of Barukh Spinoza.

faqīr (f. *faqīrah*) – 'one who is poor.' A beggar. In the Sufi context, a beggar of God, or a mature Sufi.

futuwwah – 'chivalry.'

gāthā – 'song,' 'verse.'

gāthikā – 'a sacred song' (narrative or poem).

gāthika – 'singer,' 'chanter' of a sacred song' (narrative or poem).

hadīth – 'report' or 'tradition.' A report of words or deeds of the prophet Muhammad in the Islamic tradition.

hadīth qudsī – 'holy report' or 'tradition.' A non-Qur'anic report of the words of God uttered by the prophet Muhammad, but remembered in the Islamic tradition.

Haqq – 'truth,' 'reality,' 'God-self.'

Ikhwān as-Safā' – 'brethern' or 'fellowship of purity.'

'ināyāh – kindness,' 'divine compassion.'

'ishq (alt. *'eshq)* – 'passionate love.'

'Islām – 'surrender' of 'submission' to God.

Isrā'īlīyyāt – 'of Israel,' teachings in the Islamic and Sufi traditions related to Judaism or from Jewish sources, and often applied to Christian and Zoroastrian sources as well.

jñāna yoga – 'discipline of knowledge.'

kābbālāh – 'that which is recieved,' 'tadition,' the mystical or esoteric teachings of Judaism.

kādāsh – 'to sanctify.'

kādōsh – 'holy.'

karma – 'deed,' 'action,' an action and its reciprocal consequences.

karma yoga – 'discipline of action.'

khalīfa (pl., *khulafā'*) – 'deputy' or 'steward.' A successor and representative of a *shaykh* or *murshid.*

khalwah – 'seclusion' or 'isolation.' Sufi retreat.

khānqāh (alt. *khānegāh)* – 'place' or 'traveler's house.' A building used for Sufi gatherings and dedicated to Sufi life and practice. The same as a *zāwiyah, ribat,* or *tekke.*

khirqa – 'rag' or 'cloak.' A Sufi cloak.

Khūdā – 'self-revealing,' 'God,' 'truth.'

Lā 'ilāha 'illā llāh hū – 'no god but God,' or 'there is no God; nevertheless, God.'

lata'if – 'subtleties,' or 'subtle centers' (chakras).

latifa qalbiyya – 'subtlety of the heart,' heart center' (heart chakra).

magi – Zoroastrian priests.

mahāyāna – 'great vehicle,' the second 'turning' of Buddhism.

mana – 'mind.'

mantra – 'thought' or 'sound form,' a sacred word or phrase.

maqām (pl., *maqāmāt)* – 'place' or 'station.' A level of sustained integration achieved by a Sufi, and sometimes marked by a specific role or responsibility in the Sufi community.

mukti – 'liberation' or 'release.'

muni – 'silent sage.'

murīd (f. *murīda*, pl., *murīdun)* – 'seeker.' An initiate in a Sufi lineage.

murshid (f. *murshida)* – 'guide.' The leader of a Sufi community. Parallel to *shaykh*, and sometimes *pir*.

nadir, or 'warner,' bringing a warning to the people about the way they are living, and the need for change.

najāt – 'salvation.'

nayāz – 'offering,' 'gift,' 'present.'

nirvāṇa – 'extinguished,' 'blown out,' no longer consuming the fuel of afflictive emotions and being consumed by the fires they cause.

nūr-i muhammad – 'light of Muhammad,' the perfected human ideal which existed before creation, and for which God brought everything into being.

pir-o-murshid (f. *pirnī/pirain-o-murshida)* – 'elder and guide.' In Inayati Sufism the head of an Inayati lineage.

rābita – 'bond.' The internal bond between a Sufi initiate and their master.

rāja yoga – 'royal discipline,' discipline of meditation.

risāla – 'message.'

rasūl (pl. rusul) – 'mesenger.'

safā – 'pure.'

sāhib-i safā – 'knights of purity.'

sālik (f. sālika, pl., sālikun) – 'traveler.' One who walks the spiritual path, or a competent Sufi.

samādhi – 'held-together,' one-pointed meditative absorption.

shāh – 'monarch.'

shaykh (f. shaykha, pl., shuyūkh) – 'elder.' The leader of a Sufi community, parallel to pir and murshid.

sophia – 'wisdom.'

sophos – 'sage.'

sūf – 'wool.'

ṣuffah – 'bench.'

sūfiyya – 'wool wearers.' Sufis.

tālib (f. tāliba, pl., tālibun) – 'candidate.' A candidate for entry into the Sufi path.

tarīqah (pl., turuq) – 'path' or 'order.' The Sufi path, or a particular Sufi lineage.

tasawwuf – 'purification.' Sufism.

tawḥīd – 'unity.'

tawajjeh – 'facing' or 'turning the face toward,' as in God has turned the divine face to you, giving attention to you, establishing connection in the grace of that divine attention. It is also silent dwelling in the acknowledgment of such connection. Also teaching without words. participating in a silent dialogue or exchange with a holy being.

vaishnava – 'devotee of Vishnu.'

vajrayāna – 'thunderbolt vehicle,' the third tantric 'turning' of Buddhism.

varṇa – 'caste' system of the Hindu tradition

vedānta – 'end of the Veda,' the Upanishads, mystical teachings of the Vedas.

wahdat al-wujūd – 'unity of all being' or 'existence.' The radical teaching of non-duality in Sufism. In Inayati Sufism, expressed by the phrase, 'the Message.'

yaqīn – 'certainty,' 'confidence.'

Y-H-V-H – The divine name in Hebrew as represented by the initials of the four letters, *yod-heh-vav-heh*. The name means, 'being-maker.'

yogāchāra – 'yoga practice,' an influential school of Mahyana Buddhism.

yogi – 'joined,' 'connected,' 'disciplined,' a practitioner of *yoga*.

zira'a (alt. zirat) – 'cultivation.'

Index

INDEX

INDEX

INDEX

169

INDEX

INDEX

Hazrat Inayat Khan was born in Baroda, India, on July 5th, 1882. A master of Indian classical music, he gave up a brilliant career as a musician to devote himself full-time to the spiritual path. In 1910, he followed his master's direction to go to the West to "spread the wisdom of Sufism" in the United States, England, and throughout Europe. For a decade and a half, he traveled tirelessly, giving lectures and guiding an ever-growing group of Western spiritual seekers. In 1926, he returned to India and died there the following year, on February 5th, 1927. He is entombed in the precincts of the *dargah* of Hazrat Nizam ad-Din Awliya'. Today, the universalist Sufi teachings he spread continue to inspire countless people around the world, and his spiritual heirs may be found in every corner of the planet.